# ENERGY

# Cost Savings

# For Facilities

by

Corey L. Wilson

**ENERGY Cost Savings For Facilities**

*ENERGY Cost Savings For Facilities* can be purchased in bulk with exclusive discounts for educational purposes, association gifts, sales promotions, and special editions can be created to specifications. All inquiries for such can be made below.

**CLW Enterprises**
4533 Temescal Canyon Rd. # 308
Corona, CA 92883
www.CLW-Enterprises.com
CLWEnterprises@att.net
(951) 415-3002

**CLW ENTERPRISES**

Printed paperback and eBook ePUB by Ingram Spark in La Vergne, Tennessee, USA
Copyright © 2020 & 2023: First Edition December 2020; Second Edition May 2023
Published by Fratire Publishing LLC
ISBN 978-0-9994603-9-9 (Paperback)
ISBN 978-1-953319-32-6 (eBook)
ECSFF-01-PDF (pdf)
LCCN 2020920019

Special thanks for the cover design by Jenny Barroso, J20Graphics, j20graphics@gmail.com and ebook conversion by Md. Jahurul Islam at Upwork.

# Acknowledgements

To my wife Natedao Arumsri, the love and rainbow of my life! Thank you, time, and again for supporting my literary projects like this one. Without your unconditional support, this book would not be possible.

Thank you, Jim Caldwell, former California Statewide Director and Sector Navigator; Energy, Construction & Utilities System for enlisting my support with helping to reduce our state's energy and greenhouse gas emissions.

To Dean Stanberry, IFMA Board of Director, LEED AP, USGBC, and Environmental Stewardship Utilities & Sustainability Community (ESUS) member, thanks for letting me share some of this book's content in IFMA's *Facility Management Journal.*

# Author's Preface

The second, updated, and expanded edition of *Energy Cost Savings For Facilities* guidebook is designed with your busy day and heavy workload in mind. It's organized with subheadings that target the most critical energy issues your buildings and properties are likely to encounter. The content is to the point, with no lengthy explanations, because that's what the links are for in the Appendix.

If you're like me, there are times when you spend more time searching for the information you need "right now" than using it. When your time is of the essence, that's frustrating and non-productive. One of the benefits of an e-book is that you can control-click to the chapter or subheading from the table of contents in a few seconds or search by word.

Use the *Energy Cost Savings For Facilities* as a reliable source of energy saving tips, cost saving strategies, creating a sustainable energy building program, and introduction to battery energy storage systems (BESS). Energy is a significant operations cost component and reduces net profit. Any costs you shift away from energy improves your organization's finances.

Energy is a controllable cost. Don't let it control you, your facilities, and properties, and most of all your profits. Your organization's leadership is counting on you to make the most of your limited operating budget and minimize costs. Don't let them down. Be the master of your sustainable energy building plan. You have nothing to lose and a lot to gain.

To learn more about how an energy savings system, perform an energy needs analysis, and sustainable energy strategy to use BESS, solar, and/or EV charging stations for your business and facilities, schedule a free, no-obligation introductory call at (951) 415-3002, or email me at clwenterprises@att.net, or visit my website at www.clw-enterprises.com for more information.

# Contents

# 1 – An ENERGY Savings Introduction For Facilities

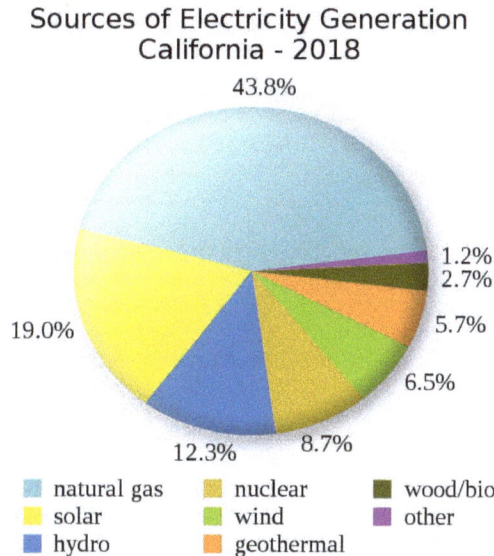

## Sources of Electricity Generation
## California - 2018

43.8%

1.2%
2.7%
5.7%
6.5%
8.7%
12.3%
19.0%

- natural gas
- solar
- hydro
- nuclear
- wind
- geothermal
- wood/bio
- other

*Credit: CPUC.*

Energy! It's one of your major cost components. It's a hot topic and will continue to be so. For most facilities and properties, the cost of energy is not going down—only up. It's essential to reduce energy costs on your building(s) whether new or existing.

Energy management is an integral part of the day-to-day operations for facility managers and property owners. Rising energy costs and increasing interest in sustainability are driving the need to reduce energy consumption in buildings and develop strategies for better management.

How energy efficient is your building? How does a facility's overall energy efficiency compare to a portfolio of buildings? Or how does it compare to other similar buildings regionally, nationwide, or internationally?

Doing more with less! That's an often-heard catch-phrase for FM's and CFO's in managing costs. The purpose of this handy guide is much the same. Energy issues can drain your budget and consume valuable resources.

Facility managers across the U.S. are focused on how clean energy can help them meet a variety of energy, economic development, and environmental goals. An early step for most energy efficiency planning involves identifying and quantifying energy savings opportunities, followed by understanding how to access this efficiency potential.

This guide is also essential for facility and property managers along with their financial officers who are serious about reducing energy usage and the cost of it to their organization's Triple Bottom Line.

## How the United States Uses Energy

Electricity and natural gas have been, and continue to be, the two dominant energy sources in the commercial buildings sector. Together electricity and natural gas accounted for about 93% of total energy consumed in 2012. Along with the increase in total electricity consumption, electricity increased its share of total energy consumed from 38% in 1979 to 61% in 2012.

Americans use a lot of energy in homes, businesses, throughout industry, and to travel and transport goods. Thirty percent of energy consumed in the commercial and industrial buildings is wasted. There are five energy-use sectors:

- The industrial sector includes facilities and equipment used for manufacturing, agriculture, mining, and construction.

- The transportation sector includes vehicles that transport people or goods, such as cars, trucks, buses, motorcycles, trains, aircraft, boats, barges, and ships.

- The residential sector includes homes and apartments.

- The commercial sector includes offices, malls, stores, schools, hospitals, hotels, warehouses, restaurants, and places of worship and public assembly.

- The electric power sector consumes primary energy to generate most of the electricity to sell to the other four sectors.

In addition to primary energy use, the industrial, transportation, residential, and commercial sectors also purchase and use most of the electricity (a secondary energy source) the electric power sector produces and sells. These four sectors are called end-use sectors because they buy or produce energy for their own consumption and not for resale.

As a result of advancements in technology, customer expectations, and state and federal policy goals, the electric power sector is evolving with increased deployment of Distributed Energy Resources (DERs). In late 2016, the Federal Energy Regulatory Commission (FERC) issued a Notice of Proposed Rulemaking (NOPR) requiring Regional Transmission Operators (RTOs) and Independent System Operators (ISOs) to facilitate the participation of electric storage resources and aggregated DERs in competitive wholesale markets.

## Energy Storage Made Record Gains in the US in 2022

Private investment in renewable energy projects hit an all-time high with over $10 billion devoted to renewable energy in the past year, Supria Ranade, head of power markets for SoftBank Group subsidiary SB Energy, told an audience at the RE+ conference in Anaheim, California.

From the Stephen Singer "Energy Storage Made Record Gains in the US in 2022" Utility Dive March 2023 article:

2

A record 4.8 GW of utility-scale non-hydropower storage was established in the U.S. in 2022, bringing total capacity to 11.4 GW, according to Sustainable Energy in America 2023 Factbook released by BloombergNEF and the Business Council for Sustainable Energy. That's up from a previous record build of 3.7 GW in 2021.

At 67%, pumped storage is the largest energy storage resource, with battery and thermal storage accounting for the remainder. Due mainly to growing deployment of large-scale lithium-ion batteries on the grid, pumped hydro's share of U.S. energy storage dropped from 78% in 2021.

Despite supply-chain related delays in project development, the U.S. remains the largest market for energy storage. Energy shifting is the dominant use case for new batteries as "pairing renewables with storage is becoming a common cost-effective option to displace fossil fuel projects," the Factbook said.

A record $141 billion in energy transition financing was deployed in the U.S. in 2022 for clean energy, including renewables, electric vehicles and other technologies, according to Factbook, which focuses on renewables, efficiency, natural gas, distributed power, storage and sustainable transportation.

It said 32 GW of new renewable power-generating capacity was added to the U.S. grid down from 37 GW commissioned in 2021 due to higher costs, trade challenges and other problems. By the end of 2022, the U.S. had 108 GWh of lithium-ion battery manufacturing commissioned. Capacity additions nearly doubled compared to 2021 with 45 GWh being added, the report said.

Utilities across the nation are beginning to cite energy-storage technologies in their long-term resource planning and as solutions to their requirements for power system flexibility.

The U.S. "made important strides" toward becoming a hub for battery manufacturing in 2022, the Factbook said. After the Inflation Reduction Act introduced a $45/kWh cell and module production tax credit, automakers and battery manufacturers have "raced to identify investment opportunities," the Factbook said.

Post- Inflation Reduction Act (IRA) commitments to the North American battery supply chain reached almost $17 billion by the end of 2022, according to the Factbook.

The IRA is expected to spur additional storage deployments. The law includes direct benefits to stationary storage deployments through a standalone investment tax credit and indirect benefits to energy storage with additional incentives for wind and solar and through battery production tax credits.

The Factbook uses BloombergNEF data in most cases, with information from the U.S. Energy Information Administration, Environmental Protection Agency, Federal Energy Regulatory Commission, American Council for an Energy-Efficient Economy, Lawrence Berkeley National

Laboratory and other sources.

## Key Takeaways of the Inflation Reduction Act (IRA)

From the "Key Takeaways of the Inflation Reduction Act (IRA) Convergent Energy + Power" August 2022 article, the recently approved $369 billion Inflation Reduction Act (IRA) is the largest and most ambitious investment in climate action that the nation has ever made and is expected to spark record-setting growth in energy storage deployment and climate change mitigation measures.

Analyst firm Wood Mackenzie noted that the IRA will bring some much-needed long-term certainty to the renewables sector with total investment in renewables reaching $1.2 trillion through 2035. According to the firm, solar will be a major beneficiary. Solar incentives in the legislation are projected to result in a "67% increase in solar additions between 2022 and 2032 compared to what would have happened without the IRA incentives."

The IRA delivers a sea change for the energy storage sector because it provides an investment tax credit that covers 30% of the size of the investment—for the first time—to what is known as "standalone" energy storage. The tax credit can increase beyond 30% with various bonuses, including those tied to developing projects in low-income communities or using US-made products. Prior, energy storage was only eligible for the investment tax credit when paired with solar, also known as solar-plus-storage.

Tax incentives and declining costs have propelled renewable energy development for over a decade, taking wind and solar from novel technologies to some of the fastest growing sources of new electricity in the nation's power grid. The foundation of energy storage's meteoric rise is attributed in part to its eligibility for current tax credits when charged by a solar array, prompting the industry to develop solar-paired storage projects. With the passage of the IRA, energy storage is finally incentivized on its own.

Before the IRA, energy storage made sense in locations where power is more expensive, including New York, California, and New England. The IRA makes sustainable power cheaper everywhere in the United States and, not only that, it creates the regulatory certainty that's needed for the private sector to invest more heavily in the clean energy transition.

### Why is it so Critical to Incentivize Energy Storage?

Energy storage is the linchpin of the clean energy transition. The more renewable energy on the grid, the better—but these resources only produce power when the sun is shining, or the wind is blowing. Energy storage can "firm up" renewable resources, maximizing their value to the grid.

But energy storage has additional value beyond pairing it with renewable resources. Energy storage can reduce the cost of electricity, by storing energy when it is cheapest and discharging the system when energy is most expensive. This can help communities and businesses save costs and carbon emissions at the same time.

In addition, energy storage can increase the reliability of our aging electric grid increasingly strained by climate change, alleviate the need for costly grid upgrades, and provide wholesale market services.

**Incentives for Renewables and Energy Storage: Understanding the IRA**

With the Inflation Reduction Act (IRA), policy resources such as the Investment Tax Credit (ITC) and Production Tax Credit (PTC) will allow developers to continue to derive partial tax exemption either annually or as some function of the energy they produce, respectively. The credits have been factored into business models across the industry, allowing projects to be deployed cost-effectively and passing greater benefits along to the communities that host them.

Legislators know that tax incentives for the technologies alone won't alleviate the logjam in renewable energy deployment, and are using the IRA to drive other policy priorities. In order to capture the "full" advertised value of the tax credits developers must provide prevailing wages and apprenticeships, in effect using present projects to nurture the clean energy workforce of the future. Additive value to a project's possible tax credits is provided to developers using domestic steel, iron, and other products.

This driver, paired with a new "advanced manufacturing production" tax credit available to domestic producers of wind turbines, solar panels, battery cells, and other grid technologies, will better secure the renewable energy supply chain from geopolitical swings, bolster the United States' manufacturing industry and its workforce, and institute higher cybersecurity and reliability standards for system components.

Other provisions will point renewable energy in areas where their depressive effect on energy costs can drive greater benefits, such as in low-income communities and those previously home to coal-fired generation, coal mines, or brownfields.

**A Sea Change for Energy Storage and Our Climate: The Expected Impact of the IRA**

Enabling our economy and society to decarbonize must be a national priority. The Inflation Reduction Act (IRA) presents our country with a greater opportunity than ever before to create and grow American jobs while also scaling domestic energy storage.

Importantly, the IRA provides the renewables community with the regulatory certainty to make long-term investments in the clean energy transition that we urgently need. The IRA cements America's leadership in the face of a crisis that has been ignored for too long. We have been seeing how important climate and decarbonization are to the investment community for several years now, and it is gratifying to see that lawmakers similarly understand their massive importance.

The renewable energy policies in the IRA foster innovation and create a level playing field to compete, and we believe this will greatly benefit the U.S. economy and our planet. We're extremely proud that the country taking this step toward decarbonization.

The United States is expected to double its manufacturing capacity by 2025, with more than 10 new battery manufacturing plants expected to be operational in the next five years. As of 2020, U.S. capacity of global electric vehicle (EV) lithium-ion cell manufacturing was approximately 59

GWh. That number is expected to grow to 224 GWh by 2025. To keep up with this demand and retain a competitive manufacturing base, the United States needs a robust supply chain and skilled workforce to produce state-of-the-art, reliable EV and grid storage batteries at scale.

Per Jennifer M. Granholm, Secretary, U.S. Department of Energy, "American leadership in the global battery supply chain will be based not only on our innovative edge, but also on our skilled workforce of engineers, designers, scientists, and production workers."

# 2 – California's Aggressive Zero Net ENERGY Goals

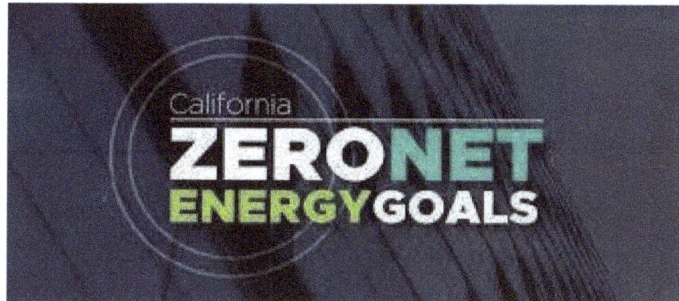

Between 2011 and 2017, California's electricity prices rose five times faster than they did nationally. Today, Californians pay 60 percent more, on average, than the rest of the nation, for residential, commercial, and industrial electricity.

California's high penetration of intermittent renewables such as solar and wind are likely a key factor in higher prices. Economists agree that "the dominant policy driver in the electricity sector [in California] has unquestionably been a focus on developing renewable sources of electricity generation."

High levels of renewable energy penetration make electricity expensive around the world, not just in California. As Germany deployed high levels of renewables over the last 10 years it saw its electricity prices rise 34 percent. Today, German electricity costs twice as much as that in neighboring France.

## California's Renewable Portfolio Standard (RPS) Increases Electricity Costs

As per the "California's Renewable Portfolio Standard (RPS) Increases Electricity Costs" Mark Nelson and Michael Shellenberger article published in Environmental Progress in February 2018: California's renewable portfolio standard (RPS) increases electricity costs in part by requiring the purchase of renewables even when they cannot be relied on to power the grid, requiring undiminished capacity from the combination of natural gas, hydro, and nuclear power.

RPS, also referred to as renewable electricity standards (RES), are policies designed to increase the use of renewable energy sources for electricity generation. These policies require or encourage electricity suppliers to provide their customers with a stated minimum share of electricity from eligible renewable resources. Although national RPS or other clean energy policies have been proposed, no federal RPS or similar policy is currently in place. However, most states have enacted their own RPS programs.

As a result, California today has a large amount of excess electricity generating capacity (the 'Duck Curve') without being able to know if much of it will be available from day to day and week to week as detailed in Chapter 12.

**As Wind and Solar Capacity Climbs, Returns of Usable Power Diminish**

As wind and solar capacity climbs, the returns of usable power diminish because of increasing curtailment during surges that the grid cannot absorb. More and more intermittent capacity has to be pushed onto the grid to get less and less additional renewable electricity. The dynamic of soaring overcapacity and falling prices is the inevitable result of the fundamental inability of intermittent wind and solar generators to efficiently match supply to demand.

The burden of higher cost electricity and benefits of renewable energy subsidies fall unevenly on Californians. Between 2007 and 2014, the highest-income 40 percent of California households received three times more in solar subsidies—valued between $10,000 and $20,000 per household—as the lowest-income 40 percent. California households with over $100,000 in annual income benefitted from energy efficiency subsidies at twice the rate of households whose income was under $50,000.

Most recently, PG&E requested a rate increase in its General Rate Case application (A18-12-009) for 2020, 2021 and 2022. Under their proposal, base rates would increase by $1,058 million or 12.4% for 2020 with subsequent increase of $454 million and $486 million for 2021 and 2022.

# Electricity Use Would Surge Under California's New Climate Plan

California's sweeping climate plan has been criticized by environmentalists for too slowly phasing out fossil fuels and relying too much on technologies to remove or capture emissions, while the oil and gas industry has said the ramp-up of clean energy is too ambitious.

Per the "Electricity Use Would Surge Under California's New Climate Plan" article by Nadia Lopez at CalMatters in June 2022: To achieve the plan's goals, air board officials project that California will need about 30 times more electric vehicles on the road, six times more electric appliances in homes to replace gas appliances, 60 times more hydrogen supply and four times more wind and solar generation capacity.

The plan "is very, very aggressive in terms of the deployment of clean technology," said Rajinder Sahota, the Air Resources Board's deputy executive officer for climate change and research. "If we can actually make all of these things happen, there are significant reductions in fossil fuel and methane that we would see by 2045. All of it hinges on implementation and successful deployment of that energy infrastructure and technology."

To handle the surge in electricity demand, air board staff said the state needs to expedite the construction of new solar and wind infrastructure, improve existing power lines and build battery storage capacity. In addition, California will need backup dispatchable power to account for energy losses when renewables like wind and solar can't produce electricity due to changes in weather.

Without these major improvements and investments, California would have to keep relying on climate-warming fossil fuels, particularly natural gas. An additional 10 gigawatts of natural gas capacity would be needed by 2045 to support the power grid if sufficient renewable power is not available by then, air board officials said.

Secretary for Environmental Protection Jared Blumenfeld said the permitting and approval process of renewable energy projects needs to be accelerated to meet the state's climate targets.

## Can California Meet Its Zero Net Energy 2045 Requirements?

From the PSE article "Net Zero Carbon California by 2045: What Will It Take?" in October 2018, by Elena Krieger, PhD, Boris Lukanov, PhD, and Seth B.C. Shonkoff, PhD, MPH:

Back in 2018, then Governor Jerry Brown launched the Global Climate Action Summit in San Francisco by announcing a sweeping and unprecedented climate target for the state of California: full carbon neutrality by the year 2045. He simultaneously signed into law a senate bill requiring 100% of the state's electricity to be produced by zero-carbon resources by 2045. The latter act stole the headlines but is in fact the far less ambitious of the two targets: 100% renewable electricity is just one of the many building blocks needed to achieve economy-wide net zero carbon emissions.

The implication of this directive is huge: by 2045 California must eliminate, sequester, or offset any and all carbon emissions to achieve net zero emissions. The executive order is not yet binding, and the legislature now needs to codify it into laws. However, how these laws will define "net" and what pathways the state takes to reach this target have profound implications for not only the climate, but also for environmental and human health co-benefits that could accrue for communities across California.

### California's Zero Net Energy Options

Net zero means that individual sources in the state can either eliminate emissions or continue to release greenhouse gases as long as those emissions are reduced elsewhere. Emission offsets can include techniques such as increasing carbon sequestration in soils, forests, and farmland, purchasing clean electricity credits from neighboring states, or through emerging technological approaches such as the direct capture and removal of carbon from the atmosphere.

California may also consider allowing emissions within the state to be offset by carbon reductions in far-away states or even other countries. However, any in-state source that uses offsets will not only continue to emit carbon, but also health-damaging co-pollutants that are often co-emitted with it. This pollution will continue to affect surrounding communities, which disproportionately impacts low-income populations and communities of color.

Achieving carbon neutrality is a vital yet formidable challenge. Carbon reductions will hinge on the implementation of widespread energy efficiency across every sector, decarbonization of the power sector (as required in SB 100) and the electrification of cars, trucks, home heating, and other sources to run on carbon-free electricity.

Currently, only 16% of California's emissions come from the power sector, 40% from transportation and the rest from industrial, residential, commercial, agriculture and other sectors. Some emission reductions, such as from cement production, will present more challenges than others and are more likely to require some kind of offset. Some may argue that California's current cap-and-trade system should be expanded to allow for the trading of carbon credits to achieve these offsets but doing so would not necessarily ensure the reduction of localized air pollutant emissions.

**Low-Income and Disadvantaged Communities Considerations**

Brown's net zero carbon executive order appropriately requires that any climate strategy seek to reduce emissions in low-income and disadvantaged communities. The degree to which this goal is achieved, however, will depend on careful policy design to ensure that the communities currently burdened with the highest impacts from fossil fuels see real environmental and health benefits.

Furthermore, any offsets or emissions trading will require clear requirements regarding the additionality and verifiability of greenhouse gas reductions. If we plant a tree, can we guarantee that it wouldn't have been planted otherwise (is it "additional")? If we export clean electricity to neighboring states, can we ensure that any fossil fuel it displaces wouldn't have been replaced by clean electricity anyway? If we increase the amount of carbon in soils through land management techniques, can we verify that the carbon is taken up and remains in the soil? These requirements are complex, particularly if out-of-state offsets with limited direct oversight are allowed.

Brown's target for carbon neutrality in 2045 and net negative emissions thereafter is groundbreaking from a policy standpoint but is in perfect alignment with the scientific consensus that we will need to not only curtail greenhouse gas emissions, but actively remove carbon dioxide from the atmosphere later this century to mitigate climate change's worst impacts.

Doing so in a verifiable, additional, and equitable way will inevitably complicate this challenge, but will also give the incoming governor and legislature a unique opportunity to lead the world with a replicable framework to achieve meaningful greenhouse gas and co-pollutant reductions with direct community benefits.

## California Dilemma: Fight Climate Change and Keep on the Lights

California sees itself as a global leader in the fight against climate change. But keeping on the lights over the next five summers is likely to increase the state's greenhouse gas emissions, energy experts said per the "Calif. dilemma: Fight climate change and keep on the lights" article by Anne C. Mulkern at Climate Wire in June 2022.

The nation's most populous state faces an electricity supply crunch, with projections showing that peak demand could exceed available supplies by as much as 3,500 megawatts. That would leave as many as 3.5 million homes without power.

To address the problem, Democratic Gov. Gavin Newsom wants to spend $5.2 billion to boost reliability. Initial plans include keeping open natural gas plants that were due to be retired.

For now, state leaders should prioritize preventing blackouts over concerns about greenhouse gas emissions, said several experts. Doing so would help maintain support for long-term climate goals.

"If the public sees this year after year — shortages and blackouts and curtailment — I think there will be a lot of setback for the long-term green energy plan that everyone hopes will come to pass," said Ahmad Faruqui, energy economist formerly with the Brattle Group consulting firm. "We live in the short run. Unless we make it through the short run, we are not going to get the long run."

Since the August 2020 rolling blackouts, the state has ordered utilities to procure 11,500 MW of power and accelerate generation projects. Battery storage capacity grew twentyfold in 2.5 years. State officials also installed emergency generators and delayed planned retirement dates for existing power plants.

Even with those actions, she said, "climate impacts are outpacing our efforts and continuing to cause unprecedented stress on California's energy system, threatening reliability and [putting] Californians at risk of additional outages."

## CPUC's Vote to Slash Solar Net Metering

Up to 2022, California installed roughly 30,000 batteries compared to 200,000 solar systems. With high costs, supply chain constraints, inflation and permitting and interconnection delays and challenges, it will take years before the storage market can match the solar market.

Bernadette Del Chiaro, executive director of the California Solar & Storage Association (CALSSA) issued the following statement on the CPUC's vote to slash solar net metering titled "CALSSA Statement on CPUC's Vote to Slash Solar Net Metering" in December 2022.

Currently 1.5 million consumers use net metering, including thousands of public schools, churches, farms, and affordable housing developments, and it is the main driver of California's world-renowned rooftop solar market. As a result of net metering, working and middle class neighborhoods are just under half of the rooftop solar market and the fastest growing segment today.

In total, distributed solar energy systems have added 13 gigawatts of solar energy to the state, roughly the size of six Diablo Canyon nuclear power plants. In addition, consumers have added nearly 1 gigawatt of energy storage which played a meaningful role in keeping the lights on during recent heat waves.

Big utilities want to change the rules in their favor in order to eliminate a growing competitor, keep consumers stuck in utility monopolies, and protect their profits. Utilities claim solar makes the energy bills of non-solar customers more expensive. But in reality, utility profits, infrastructure investment, transmission lines, and paying for their bad planning and the fires they cause are what drives energy rates up. Californians are not fooled, and real equity champions know energy fairness is about "making rooftop solar panels and batteries more—not less—affordable for working families and lower-income Californians."

A proposed decision released in December 2021, that would have implemented an unprecedented solar tax and drastic net metering credit reductions, was shelved earlier this year after intense backlash and public disapproval from Governor Newsom. Despite that backlash and the overwhelming popularity of rooftop solar in California, the CPUC's revised proposed decision still included an immediate and drastic slash to the value of net metering.

With rooftop solar's vital contribution to reaching California's clean energy goals, the promise of battery storage for grid reliability, and new federal incentives for going solar, a diverse coalition of solar supporters are calling on the California leaders to keep solar growing and affordable for all types of consumers. More than 160,000 people submitted comments to the CPUC and Governor Newsom calling for a strong NEM-3 decision, the highest count in CPUC history.

# 3 – Your Facilities' Electrical ENERGY Future Is Now

*Credit: CEC*

As facility managers endeavor to reduce carbon emissions as part of their organizations' climate plan, renewables are an absolute must as noted in the *FM Prime* "What Is the Role of Renewables in Building Electrification and Efficiency?" article by Greg Zimmerman.

As energy efficiency and deep energy retrofits with the goal of net-zero energy buildings become more common for facility managers, a "which comes first, the chicken or egg" discussion has also emerged: Does a facility manager focus first on efficiency and then renewables to make up the difference? Or the other way around?

Most experts suggest this is a no-brainer: Make the facility as efficient as possible, and then cover the rest in onsite renewables. If the facility isn't efficient, even if one is still using renewables, wasted energy is wasted energy. So be as efficient as possible, use as little energy as possible, and produce the difference between the energy spent and zero with renewables.

As more and more buildings are working toward electrification, this conversation about the role of renewables in an efficient building becomes even more relevant. The foundation for the goal of building electrification is that buildings will be using renewable energy, and therefore greatly reducing or eliminating fossil fuels (like natural gas) from buildings altogether. The two strategies must be complementary to ensure that both are effective.

Renewables are crucial because they get buildings closer to zero carbon aligned, which will be necessary to reach global and U.S. climate goals. The inverse of this question might yield more insight into the momentum we need to retrofit a largely inefficient and aging building stock.

Why are deep energy retrofits crucial to generating clean energy for our buildings? Poorly performing buildings, even with renewables, will require significant energy load supply from existing grid infrastructure.

Renewable energy and high-performing buildings that are energy efficient go hand-in-hand by minimizing energy loads and making clean energy go even further. Whether or not a building is compatible with onsite solar or other renewables, every facility manager can play their part by reducing their energy load and improving overall efficiency.

Per Ella Mure, an associate with RMI's Carbon-Free Buildings Program, direct lifecycle costing highlights the significant return on investment for renewables. These options drastically cut operating costs in the long run, and the payback towards the upfront costs is happening quickly. As utility prices continue to vary and increase over time, onsite renewables are the best way to control costs and reduce the risk of unpredictable and variable utility rates.

Solar investment tax credits can provide significant federal tax credits for building owners, plus whatever local and state credits are available. Solar loans or leases are another financing opportunity property owners can explore. This involves a lease or loan provided by a bank (the lender can partner with an energy service company) for solar systems, including battery storage, where the lessor owns the solar equipment, and the customer leases the solar system. In this case, the equipment ownership reverts to the building owner at the lease payoff.

Power purchasing agreements (PPA) are another financing mechanism where a developer designs, permits, and installs an energy system on a customer's property at little to no cost and then sells the power generated to the customer at a fixed per kWh below retail rate.

## Energy Storage Will Have Its Biggest Year Yet

As utilities plan to decarbonize their systems, many see the current boom in natural gas generation as a "bridge" to a low-carbon future providing dispatchable power to balance out intermittent renewables on their systems. Continued advancements in battery technology, however, could make that bridge shorter than many anticipated.

In November 2018, California regulators approved four battery projects for utility Pacific Gas & Electric (PG&E) to replace three gas plants that had sought ratepayer financial support. The batteries, including two of the world's largest planned projects, represented the first time that a utility and its regulators sought to directly replace multiple major power plants with battery storage.

California has ambitious environmental and battery storage targets, but large-scale storage is also spreading to states without those policies as battery prices decline. Last summer, generator Vistra announced plans for a 42 MWh storage facility connected to a solar farm in Texas, which would be the state's largest battery.

While smaller in scale, the recent growth in utility-size batteries has been outpaced by behind-the-meter installations, which analysis firm Wood Mackenzie says grew more than 300% in 2017 alone. Going forward, Bloomberg analysts expect lower prices and increasing market participation options for storage like FERC's recently approved Orders 841 and 2222 will beget more than 100 GWh of storage capacity in the U.S. alone by 2040.

### Lithium-ion Battery Costs Continue to Drop

BNEF's Energy Storage Outlook *2019*, predicts a further halving of lithium-ion battery costs per kilowatt-hour by 2030, as demand takes off in two different markets – stationary storage and electric vehicles. The report goes on to model the impact of this on a global electricity system increasingly penetrated by low-cost wind and solar.

Just 10 countries are on course to represent almost three quarters of the global market in gigawatt terms, according to BNEF's forecast. South Korea is the lead market in 2019, but will soon cede that position, with China and the U.S. far in front by 2040. The remaining significant markets include India, Germany, Latin America, Southeast Asia, France, Australia and the U.K.

In the USA, a review of compliance filings submitted by grid operators in response to the Federal Energy Regulatory Commission's (FERC) Orders 841 and 2222 show that Independent System Operators (ISOs) and Regional Transmission Organizations (RTOs) are complying with FERC's directive, but work remains to be done.

### Distributed Energy Resources (DERs)

Utilities, keen to prevent load loss to rooftop solar and the like, initially tried to slow the trend with fees and rate designs that discouraged adoption of such resources. But increasingly—and after a series of lengthy state policy battles—they are beginning to recognize that Distributed Energy Resources (DERs) can also provide benefits to the grid and if managed correctly, will become a reliable Behind the Meter (BTM) power resource.

California Independent System Operators (CAISO) refers to storage as a "vital strategy" to meet California's goal of 100% zero-carbon electricity by 2045. The state's current oversupply of solar power in the middle of the day and subsequent drop-off in the evening has led to a curtailment of solar. With more storage on the grid, the oversupply of solar could be captured and used later in the day, reducing the need for curtailment and increasing the grid operator's ability to balance load, CAISO said.

## Electric Vehicle (EV) Growth Will Become an Energy Demand Issue

As batteries become cheaper they hold promise for utilities not just as stationary sources of power, but mobile ones as well. By 2050, the National Renewable Energy Laboratory says electric vehicles could increase U.S. power demand by up to 38%, providing an important source of power demand growth for utilities and opportunities to use the vehicles' batteries to meet grid needs.

In 2018, utilities began to realize this opportunity, ramping up their lobbying and public relations efforts around electric vehicles. In the third quarter alone, 32 states and D.C. took some action on electric vehicles, including the approval of utility EV charging programs in Massachusetts, Rhode Island and, earlier, in Nevada.

In the years to come, utilities across the nation are likely to intensify these efforts, pushing for approval to own EV charging stations, studying new rate designs to incentivize charging, and finding new ways to aggregate fleets of vehicles to modulate their charging for grid needs.

**EV's Could Overwhelm the Nation's Grids**

The power demand from the 20 million electric vehicles (EVs) expected to be on U.S. roads by 2030, up from today's 1.1 million, could overwhelm the nation's grids.

However, the coming EV load could deliver great value to utilities and their customers if it is shifted away from high-priced peak demand periods. That would increase utilities' electricity sales without adding stress to their grids, while also lowering drivers' charging costs. Investing in the communications systems and planning needed to properly manage charging can deliver transportation electrification's full value, stakeholders told Utility Dive.

EVs are the biggest "electric load opportunity for utilities" since the 1950s air conditioning explosion, a May 2019 Smart Electric Power Alliance (SEPA) study reports. But without proper planning to integrate that load, "EVs could lead to grid constraints and increased transmission and distribution peaks" that require new "peaker plants, unplanned grid upgrades, and other costly solutions."

"There is already adequate charging infrastructure technology to incorporate real-time pricing and use price signals to shift charging from peak demand periods to times when utilities have renewables over-generation," the report adds.

**What's Coming for EV Energy Storage**

The threat to the grid represented by EV growth will not be due to a lack of the Electric Vehicle Supply Equipment (EVSE) used for charging. An estimated 9.6 million EV charging ports will be needed by 2030, according to the Edison Electric Institute, but 2018's 1.2 million North American charging ports will grow ten times to over 12.6 million by 2027, according to Navigant.

With the electrification of trains, trucks, buses and other vehicles, the coming load could be overwhelming. "But worst-case scenarios assume transportation electrification would happen without optimizing the grid, and there are ways to optimize. Managing the number of cars charging, and when they charge, will determine the real load."

## Wind, Solar to Make Up 70% of New US Generating Capacity While Batteries Gain Momentum

Wind and solar will represent more than two-thirds of new electric generating capacity to come online in 2021, while battery storage capacity is set to quadruple over the next year, according to the U.S. Energy Information Administration (EIA).

Per the "Wind, Solar to Make Up 70% of New US Generating Capacity in 2021 While Batteries Gain Momentum" article content courtesy of Emma Penrod at Utility Dive in January 2021: Two-thirds of new solar projects are now built in tandem with energy storage, according to Sam Newell, a principal analyst for The Brattle Group.

At current pace, wind, solar and storage could overtake conventional technologies as the leading source of generation by the early 2030s, according to Wood Mackenzie principal analyst

Robert Whaley.

Renewable energy is still a ways from becoming the dominant source of energy on the U.S. electric grid, but wind and solar will remain the resources of choice for new development in 2021.

According to EIA, the U.S. is set to bring 39.7 GW of new capacity online by the end of 2021. Natural gas generation will represent just over 16% of this new capacity, according to EIA, with 6.6 GW scheduled to come online this year. Wind generation is expected to grow 12.2 GW — down from 21 GW in 2020.

Solar, meanwhile, will enjoy another record-breaking year, with 15.4 GW in new capacity expected to come online in 2021. The U.S. is also expected to add 4.3 GW of battery storage, more than quadrupling existing capacity, according to EIA.

**The Growth of Solar is Bringing the Storage Sector With It**

The growth of solar, Sam Newell said, is in many ways bringing the storage sector along with it. While there are standalone battery projects, he said, the industry has made a rapid pivot to solar-plus-storage as the preferred format, with two-thirds of solar projects already coupled with batteries. Wind is paired with storage much less frequently, he said.

The 2021 trends identified by EIA have been in the works for some time — renewable energy deployment has outnumbered new conventional development since roughly 2015. But Newell the speed with which renewable energy has overtaken conventional generation assets has far exceeded expectations.

"This has been going on for several years," he said, and while wind is expected to see a decline this year, renewable energy resources overall continue to grow. "They're blowing past what we once thought would be the saturation point for such intermittent resources."

Newell attributed this explosive growth to rapid declines in the cost of renewable energy — declines far outpacing improvements seen in conventional technologies, and even some of the most optimistic estimates for how quickly renewable energy would become affordable. But policy also played a role, he said, and the regions which have seen the most rapid deployment of renewable energy are also those that set early, ambitious goals for renewable energy.

The incoming Biden administration, Newell said, could prompt even greater renewable energy deployment if lawmakers implement measures such as a national carbon policy or renewable energy standard.

"That would bring in some of the states where it's not much cheaper to do the renewables, and that don't have the environmental mandates," he said.

Even without any change in policy, Whaley said, the current rate of renewable energy deployment will see wind and solar overtaking fossil fuels as the source of the majority of U.S. energy by the early 2030s. Wood Mackenzie expects the renewable sector will continue to enjoy incremental growth through roughly the same time period, with growth beginning to stabilize around 2033.

"Certainly all the momentum is for renewables, and they're dominating additions," he said, "but it's still going to take a while for solar and wind to overtake gas."

However, because wind, geothermal, biomass and other renewable energy systems are not typically options for most building structures like solar, battery storage and EV charging stations are, they are not cover in this guidebook. Covering a rooftop with PV panels is possible but mounting a wind turbine on a building's roof top is not.

The same goes for hydro, thermal, biomass and other renewable energy sources that a typical building cannot be equipped for. There are too many structural, special and/or code compliant issues and restrictions to overcome.

# 4 – Battery ENERGY Storage Systems For Facilities

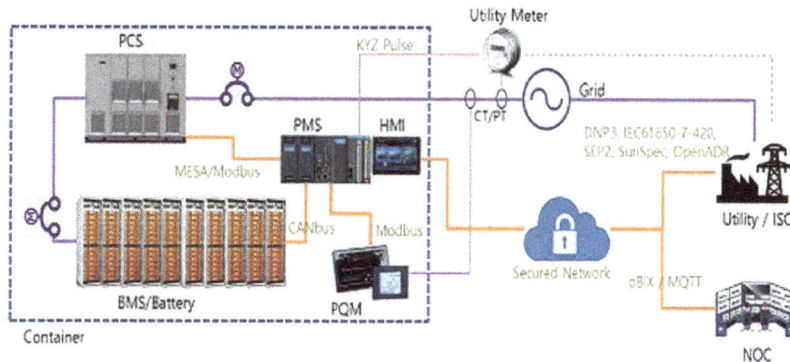

*Credit: MicroNOC Inc.*

The market for solar has grown quickly over the last decade, but ultimately, to tap into the full value of solar energy, businesses need a way to control the timing of that energy use. The best way to do that is with energy storage.

It's pretty simple: Solar energy produced during the day gets stored inside batteries for later use. When the solar production goes down in the late afternoon and time-based rates spike upward, businesses can draw energy from the batteries rather than paying for expensive power from the grid. Businesses can also use power from the batteries when their energy demand is highest to lower their demand charges.

Energy storage installations around the world will multiply exponentially, from a modest 9GW/17GWh deployed as of 2018 to 1,095GW/2,850GWh by 2040, according to the latest forecast from research company BloombergNEF (BNEF).

This 122-fold boom of stationary energy storage over the next two decades will require $662 billion of investment, according to BNEF estimates. It will be made possible by further sharp declines in the cost of lithium-ion batteries, on top of an 85% reduction in the 2010-18 period.

As new rooftop solar and battery storage systems evolved, the technology to aggregate their extra energy capacity Behind-the-Meter (BTM) and distribute it back to the power grid has arrived. It's called Distributed Energy Resources (DERs) and it offers utilities the opportunity to meet bulk power sector needs by utilizing their smaller customers who have extra energy reserves to transfer back to the electrical distribution grid.

Until 2019, DER technology moved faster than federal, state and power / gird supplier / operator regulations. In California, now that FERC, CAISO, SCE, PG&E, SDG&E and the California Public Utilities Commission (CPUC) agencies energy regulations are completed and in place, the private BTM aggregators can fully integrate into California's energy markets and offer commercial and industrial facility managers (FM's) substantial savings.

More precisely, a facility or portfolio of buildings can benefit as a distributed energy resource DER if managed effectively by a Battery Energy Saving System (BESS) that lowers their energy usage and in turn reduces their operating costs.

A BESS can manage and regulate energy usage by purchasing it at the lowest peak usage rates and releasing it when energy demand is at its highest. They also prevent energy spikes and excessive energy demand by modulating and flattening energy usage for peak performance. As more loads and generating resources are connected through DERs, power usage will decrease, outages will cease, and this nascent industry will graduate to a full-fledge grid resource, which is ready to happen.

The commercial and residential need for rooftop solar, electric vehicles and now battery storage shows no sign of slowing down and will accelerate to meet our nation's growing electrical requirements that are replacing non-renewable resources like coal, petroleum and natural gas.

## What is Energy Storage?

Energy can be stored in batteries for when it is needed. The battery energy storage system definition is an advanced technological solution that allows energy storage in multiple ways for later use.

Given the possibility that an energy supply can experience fluctuations due to weather, blackouts, or for geopolitical reasons, battery systems are vital for utilities, businesses and homes to achieve a continual power flow. A battery energy storage system (BESS) is no longer an afterthought or an add-on, but rather an important pillar of any energy strategy.

### What is Solar Energy Storage?

A solar energy storage system is a technological solution in which batteries charge during the day when the sun is shining, and store and release power for consumption around the clock or on cloudy days. Battery energy storage is particularly effective when combined with solar energy because solar energy storage mitigates the intermittent nature of renewable power and guarantees a steady supply of electricity.

Modern batteries for a home or business solar energy system usually include a built-in inverter to change the DC current generated by solar panels into the AC current needed to power appliances or equipment. Solar battery storage works with an energy management system that manages the charge and discharge cycles based on real-time needs and availability.

## Battery Energy Storage Solutions

Battery storage can be used in many ways that go beyond the simple emergency backup in the event of an energy shortage or blackout. Applications differ depending on whether the storage is being used for a business or a home.

The Enel X website provides a great outline of "What is Energy Storage?" for commercial and industrial users, and shows us there are several applications:

- Peak shaving, or the ability to manage energy demand to avoid a sudden short term spike in consumption.

- Load shifting, which allows businesses to shift their energy consumption from one time period to another, by tapping the battery when energy costs more.

- Flexibility, whereby customers can reduce their site's grid demand at critical times – without changing their electricity consumption. Energy storage therefore makes it a lot easier to participate in a Demand Response program and save on energy costs.

- Microgrids rely on batteries as a key component because these grids need energy storage to enable them to disconnect from the main electricity grid when needed.

- Integration with renewable energy sources since batteries guarantee a smooth and continuous electricity flow in the absence of the availability of power from renewable.

**What Are the Battery Energy Storage Benefits?**

The advantages of battery storage systems are many. They make renewable energy more reliable and thus more viable. The supply of solar and wind power can fluctuate, so battery storage systems are crucial to "smoothing out" this flow to provide a continuous power supply of energy when it's needed around the clock, no matter whether the wind is blowing or the sun is shining. Plus, they can protect any user from grid fluctuations that could compromise energy supply. Here are some of the advantages of battery storage:

- Environmental gains: Installing a battery storage system in a home or businesses powered by renewable energy reduces pollution, thereby contributing to the energy transition and combating the effects of global warming.

- Lower energy costs: Storing low-cost energy and consuming it during peak periods when electricity rates are higher allows a user to shift consumption and avoid higher charges, saving money. The savings are magnified when combined with solar power, which is free.

- Less dependent on the grid: Battery storage systems guarantee a continuous energy supply, even at times when the energy grid is unstable due to peaks in demand or extreme weather.

- "Always on" supply: The sun is not always "on." A battery storage system works round the clock, and therefore compensates for any fluctuations in solar energy supply by storing any excess power in the system.

- Resilience: A battery storage system provides emergency backup in the event of a power outage, guaranteeing business continuity.

### How Does a Battery Storage System Work?

The operating principle of a battery energy storage system (BESS) is straightforward. Batteries receive electricity from the power grid, straight from the power station, or from a renewable energy source like solar panels or other energy source, and subsequently store it as current to then release it when it is needed.

When combined with software, a BESS becomes a platform that couples the energy storage capacity of batteries with the intelligence needed to deliver advanced management of energy consumption by harnessing AI, machine learning and data-driven solutions. This makes batteries a tool in the effort to offset climate change, because they enable a more flexible way of using energy that lets the user adapt to dips and peaks in demand and supply.

Overall, battery energy storage systems foster the deployment of renewable sources, thereby helping reduce carbon emissions and even deliver lower costs for businesses and households.

### Which Are the Different Meter Systems for Battery Energy Storage?

A battery energy storage system (BESS) can be of two types: front-of-the-meter (FTM) or behind-the-meter (BTM). BTM systems are installed on the user's premises and are typically smaller than a FTM system.

A BTM's main function is to improve the stability of its owners energy supply and cut costs, but if the local regulatory framework allows for it, the batteries can also supply energy back into the grid and thereby become an additional revenue stream.

The larger FTM systems are directly connected to the power grid and usually therefore belong to a utility, helping it solve network congestion issues or as an alternative to building new power lines.

### How Long Does a Battery Energy Storage Last and How to Give It a Second Life?

Most energy battery storage systems last between 5 to 15 years. As part of the ecosystem of solutions for the energy transition, battery energy storages are tools to enable sustainability and, at the same time, they themselves must be fully sustainable.

The reuse of batteries and recycling of the materials they contain at the end of their life are all-around sustainability goals and an effective application of Circular Economy principles. Recovering an increasing quantity of materials from batteries and giving them a second life leads to environmental benefits, in both the extraction and disposal stages. Battery reuse also delivers economic benefits.

## BNEF's Energy Storage Outlook

The BloombergNEF (BNEF) energy storage outlook 2019, titled "Energy Storage Investments Boom As Battery Costs Halve in the Next Decade" predicts a further halving of lithium-ion battery costs per kilowatt-hour by 2030, as demand takes off in two different markets – stationary storage and electric vehicles. The report goes on to model the impact of this on a global electricity system increasingly penetrated by low-cost wind and solar.

BNEF's analysis suggests that cheaper batteries can be used in more and more applications. These include energy shifting (moving in time the dispatch of electricity to the grid, often from times of excess solar and wind generation), peaking in the bulk power system (to deal with demand spikes), as well as for customers looking to save on their energy bills by buying electricity at cheap hours and using it later.

Logan Goldie-Scot, head of energy storage at BNEF, added: "In the near term, renewables-plus-storage, especially solar-plus-storage, has become a major driver for battery build. This is a new era of dispatchable renewables, based on new contract structures between developer and grid."

**Ten Countries Represent Almost Three Quarters of the Global Market**

In gigawatt terms, according to BNEF's forecast, just 10 countries are on course to represent almost three quarters of the global market in gigawatt terms, according to BNEF's forecast. South Korea is the lead market in 2019, but will soon cede that position, with China and the U.S. far in front by 2040. The remaining significant markets include India, Germany, Latin America, Southeast Asia, France, Australia, and the U.K.

There is a fundamental transition developing in the power system and transportation sector. Falling wind, solar and battery costs mean wind and solar are set to make up almost 40% of world electricity in 2040, up from 7% today. Meanwhile passenger electric vehicles could become a third of the global passenger vehicle fleet by 2040, up from less than half a percent today, adding huge scale to the battery manufacturing sector.

**Demand for Energy Storage Will Increase Dramatically**

The demand for energy storage will increase to balance the higher proportion of variable, renewable generation in the electricity system. Electrical storage batteries paired with Energy Storage Systems (ESS), will increasingly be chosen to manage this dynamic supply and demand mix.

The report finds that energy storage will become a practical alternative to new-build electricity generation or network reinforcement, eliminating the need for peaker plants. Behind-the-meter storage will also increasingly be used to provide system services on top of customer applications for new and existing commercial, industrial, institutional, and residential buildings.

The total demand for batteries from the stationary storage and electric transport sectors is forecast to be 4,584GWh by 2040, providing a major opportunity for battery makers and miners of component metals such as lithium, cobalt and nickel, and the countries that possess these resources.

# 5 – Potential ENERGY Cost Savings For Facilities

*Credit: Getty Images.*

EPA's ENERGY STAR Portfolio Manager program calculates that a 10 percent decrease in energy use could lead to a 1.5 percent increase in Net Operating Income (NOI) with even more impressive figures as the energy savings grow.

Using commercial real estate as an example, energy use is the single largest operating expense in commercial office buildings, representing approximately one-third of typical operating budgets and accounting for almost 20 percent of the nation's annual greenhouse gas emissions.

By becoming more energy efficient, all types of buildings from industrial, educational, hospitals, retail, warehouse and many others can reduce operating expenses, increase property asset value, and enhance the comfort of their tenants. They can also demonstrate their commitment to the environment by reducing pollution and the harmful Greenhouse Gas (GHG) emissions that contribute to global warming.

## No Cost to Low Cost Opportunities

Looking for a quick return on an energy investment? Here's a laundry list of ideas to get started with saving energy that often have a rapid payback. Complete these items first before you consider other options. The best part? These energy management best practices continue to save you money long after the initial project cost is paid off.

**Cost Effective Measures**

- Measure and track energy performance.

- Turn off lights when not in use or when natural daylight can be used.

- Set back the thermostat in the evenings and other times when a building is unoccupied.

- Educate tenants and employees about how their behaviors affect energy use.

- Improve operations and maintenance practices by regularly checking and maintaining equipment to ensure it is functioning efficiently.

- Optimize start-up time, power-down time, and equipment sequencing.

- Revise janitorial practices to reduce the hours that lights are turned on each day.

**Cost-Effective Investments**

- Use an energy management system (EMS).

- Engage in energy audits and retrocommissioning to identify areas of inefficiency.

- Install energy efficient lighting systems. ENERGY STAR qualified compact fluorescent lights prevent carbon dioxide from entering the atmosphere.

- Purchase energy-efficient products like ENERGY STAR qualified office and commercial food service equipment.

- Retrofit, upgrade, or install new heating and cooling equipment to meet reduced loads and take advantage of efficient technologies.

- Use a performance contract to guarantee energy savings from upgrades made.

- Work with an energy services provider to manage and improve performance.

- Plug air leaks with weather stripping and caulking.

## Low Cost to Medium Cost Items

If you're looking for a higher return on investment (ROI) in relation to more expenditures for energy savings products and practices, look into these solutions if your budget permits. If it doesn't, the quick payback in energy and cost savings can justify the expense.

**Lighting** (see Chapter 10 for more information)

- Replace old fluorescent and incandescent lighting with T-8 (or even T-5) fixtures, ENERGY STAR certified CFLs or LEDs, and other energy-efficient lighting systems that improve light quality and reduce heat gain. CFLs cost about 75 percent less to operate, and last about 10 times longer.

- Install LED exit signs. These signs can dramatically reduce maintenance by eliminating the need to replace lamps.

- Swap out incandescent light bulbs with ENERGY STAR certified CFLs or LEDs in your desk, task, and floor lamps.

- Install occupancy sensors to automatically turn off lights when no one is present and back on when people return. Storage rooms, back-of-house spaces, meeting rooms, and other low-traffic areas are often good places to start. Occupancy sensors can save between 15 and 30 percent on lighting costs. Before you begin, check with your local utility to see if they offer any incentives. Reference the DSIRE - Database of State Incentives for Renewables & Efficiency section in the Appendix for more information.

- Examine the opportunity to switch from high-pressure sodium lamps to metal halide lamps in parking lots and consider upgrading to LED lighting for outdoor signage.

**Food Service Equipment**

- For existing refrigerators, clean refrigerator coils twice a year and replace door gaskets and door seals as needed.

- Have large and walk-in refrigeration systems serviced at least annually. This includes cleaning, refrigerant top off, lubrication of moving parts, and adjustment of belts. This will help ensure efficient operation and longer equipment life.

- Consider retrofitting existing refrigerators and display cases with anti-sweat door heater controls, and variable speed evaporator fan motors and controls.

**Heating and Cooling** (see Chapter 11 for more information)

- Tune up your heating, ventilation, and air conditioning (HVAC) system with an annual maintenance contract. Even a new HVACR system, like a new car, will decline in performance without regular maintenance. A contract automatically ensures that your HVACR contractor will provide "pre-season" tune-ups before each cooling and heating season. Your chances of an emergency HVACR breakdown also decrease with regular maintenance.

- Install window films and add insulation or reflective roof coating to reduce energy consumption.

- Upgrade and maintain heating and cooling equipment. Replace chlorofluorocarbon chillers, retrofit or install energy-efficient models to meet a building's reduced cooling loads, and upgrade boilers and other central plant systems to energy-efficient standards.

- Use a performance contract to guarantee energy savings from upgrades made.

- Work with an energy service provider to help manage and improve energy performance.

- Retro or recommission the building to make sure it's running the way it was intended.

- Consider energy audits to identify areas where building systems have become inefficient over time and bring them back to peak performance.

## Longer Term Solutions & Larger Capital Expenditures

These larger cost and long-term investments can also generate a high return on investment (ROI) over an extended period of time. However, they're for consideration after the low no cost to mid cost energy saving ideas have been implemented. For more information for a plan to secure approval and funding for these measures, see Chapter 15 – Utilizing an ENERGY Savings Plan Budget For Facilities

### Heating and Cooling

- Install variable frequency drives (VFDs) and energy-efficient motors.

- Upgrade and maintain heating and cooling equipment. Replace chlorofluorocarbon chillers, retrofit or install energy-efficient models to meet a building's reduced cooling loads, and upgrade boilers and other central plant systems to energy-efficient standards.

- Install economizers on rooftop package units.

### Food Service Equipment

- Purchase ENERGY STAR certified commercial food service equipment.

### Office Equipment

- Purchase energy-efficient products like ENERGY STAR certified office equipment, electronics, and commercial cooking equipment.

# 6 – Sustainable ENERGY Buildings Plans For Facilities

*Credit: IFMA.*

A building can't be green if it isn't energy efficient. Why? The energy used by buildings is mostly generated by burning fossil fuels, which releases Greenhouse Gas Emissions (GHG) that contribute to climate change. No building should define itself as "green" unless it consumes less energy and generates fewer greenhouse gas emissions than average.

How can you be sure that a building is energy efficient? Many new buildings today are designed and built to be green—a very exciting trend that will pay big dividends in the future for building operators and for the environment. Most have not.

However, just because a new building is built to be green, doesn't mean it will be energy efficient. Nor will a building built before green standards were implemented—cannot be green. And even more important, buildings often don't perform the way they were designed to. It's important to rely on proven methods to ensure that buildings are designed to maximize energy efficiency, and that they actually perform as intended once they're operational.

Many building and property managers today are being asked: "What are we doing in our buildings to be more sustainable?" Whether it's determining your current status towards being more sustainable, or how you can save money in your building's operations by being more energy efficient or taking you through a building rating system certification—the answers on how to effectively manage your facilities and properties using sustainable practices to are not always on hand and easily accessible—until now.

An in depth study performed by the International Facility Management Association (IFMA) members, primarily FM's, revealed that most have implemented a variety of sustainable practices. However, the majority does not have a master plan in implementation but rather selectively choose different sustainable practices. Many are familiar with the term "green design," but were not as familiar with the LEED rating system or environmentally preferable purchasing. The facility managers in this study consider projects to be sustainable if they:

- Use a minimal level of energy to operate.
- Have a lower total environmental impact.
- Have fewer harmful emissions.
- Contain products that are easily recycled.
- Use products manufactured in an environmentally friendly way.
- Have products made from recycled products.

## What is a Sustainable Energy Buildings Plan (SEBP)

A Sustainable Energy Buildings Plan (SEBP) optimizes Energy Storage Systems (ESS) and efficient energy management in support of the primary purpose of the organization. A SEBP has the potential to manage energy resources in a manner consistent with all that is green, zero-net-energy and high-performance.

The idea of sustainable energy is not just about doing something that is environmentally or people-friendly. It's about that, but it's also about making facilities last, perform at a level that meets the needs of the organization, managed in a manner that is consistent with the mission, vision, and values of the organization, and most of all, lowering energy usage.

Energy saving performance characteristics include; energy efficiency, low reliance on natural resources, low-carbon, and a healthier indoor environment. The term "high-performance" fits well into the facility manager's lexicon because it basically describes an outcome that facility and property managers have been seeking since long before buildings were termed "green." Their goal has always been to optimize performance while saving energy.

## Starting a Sustainable Energy Buildings Plan (SEBP)

The challenge with successfully incorporating energy saving practices is often found within the organizational culture. Change is not easily accepted and "business as usual" seems to be the motto when new ideas or methods are introduced. However, in any organization, at any point in time, change is necessary and will more than likely require a gradual, result-driven integration.

Today, sustainable energy management is not the sole responsibility of one department; it must become a part of the organizational culture. At all levels within an organization, there are lessons to be shared with regard to the synergy between sustainability and energy management. In order to ddevelop a successful SEBP, the following needs to happen:

- Identify the impact of existing facilities on people, the environment, and the finances of the organization, known as the Triple Bottom Line (TBL).

- Understand Total Cost of Ownership (TCO), Return on Investment (ROI), and Life-Cycle Costing (LCC).

- Determine if your organization's mission statement includes Corporate Social Responsibility (CSR) which is the commitment to contribute to economic development while improving the quality of life of the workforce and their families as well as of the community and society at large.

- Align the facility and property management strategies with the organization's commitment to the TBL and CSR efforts.

- Create a strategy for delivering sustainable energy management.

- Secure senior management buy-in and/or a policy champion to make it happen.

- Create a process for measuring and monitoring energy, resources, use and savings.

- Develop a change management strategy and communications plan to engage your workforce in sustainable energy management.

## Energy Use Intensity (EUI) is the Key Performance Indicator (KPI)

The key performance indicator (KPI) for a SEBP is the Energy Use Intensity (EUI) metric. When using EUI, energy use is expressed as a function of a building's total area or "footprint" or other characteristics. In the United States, EUI is typically expressed in energy used per square foot of building footprint per year. It is calculated by dividing the total gross energy consumed in a one-year period (expressed in kilowatt-hours or kilo-British Thermal Units) by the total gross square footage of the building.

**Calculating a Building's EUI**

Example: A school contains a main floor consisting of 15,000 square feet, a second floor consisting of 10,500 square feet. The school used 1,170,000 kilowatt-hours of power during the year in question. Kilowatt-hours is multiplied by 3.412 to obtain kBTUs, therefore 1,170,000 x 3.412 = 3,992,040 kBTUs. This is divided by the total square footage of 25,500 square feet for an Energy Use Intensity of 3,992,040 / 22,500 = 156.5 kBTU/sf.

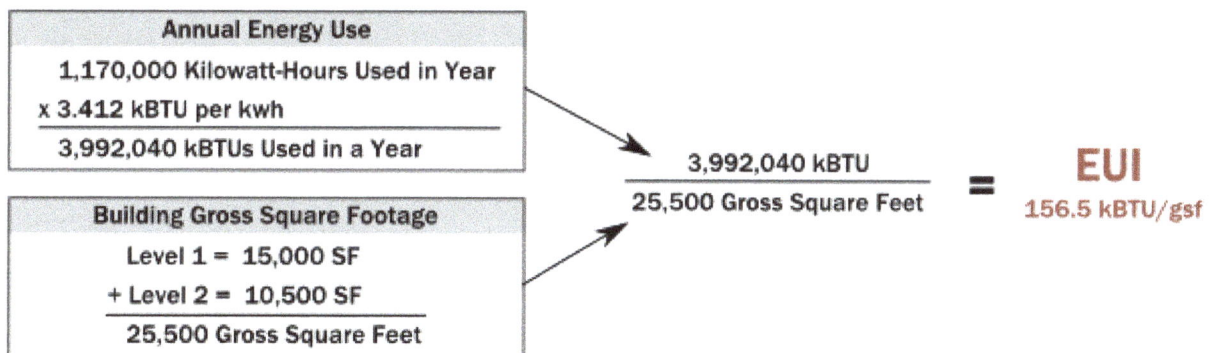

| **Annual Energy Use** |
| --- |
| 1,170,000 Kilowatt-Hours Used in Year |
| x 3.412 kBTU per kwh |
| 3,992,040 kBTUs Used in a Year |

| **Building Gross Square Footage** |
| --- |
| Level 1 = 15,000 SF |
| + Level 2 = 10,500 SF |
| 25,500 Gross Square Feet |

$$\frac{3,992,040 \text{ kBTU}}{25,500 \text{ Gross Square Feet}} = \text{EUI} \quad 156.5 \text{ kBTU/gsf}$$

## What Affects a Building's EUI?

EUI can vary significantly depending on building type. Hospitals have EUIs that can range from 400 to 500 kBTU/sf, due the high energy demand of interior lighting and hospital equipment. In contrast, a school may have an EUI in the range of 150 kBTU/sf. Food services facilities tend to have very high energy usage, and can have EUIs in the range of 800 kBTU/sf.

Climate can have a significant effect on EUI, due to the variations in heating and cooling costs between different areas of the country. For this reason, EUI values may be broken up into region to provide a more accurate comparison of selected structures, or the values may be "weather-normalized" to adjust the EUI to be compared against a building in a different type of climate.

The US Energy Information Administration (EIA) compiles information via the Commercial Buildings Energy Consumption Survey (CBECS) that allow for a comparison of energy consumption based on building sizes and types of use. EIA has set energy use reduction challenge targets for the year 2030 that comprise energy use reductions of 70%, regardless of building type or use.

**Reduction of Energy Use Intensity (EUI)**

Some of the methods used to reduce energy use intensity are:

- Ensuring proper maintenance of equipment to improve efficiency of operation.

- Installing motion activated lights (occupancy sensors).

- Incorporate the use of natural sunlight into the design of occupied spaces.

- Provide a means for passive heating and cooling of interior spaces.

- Develop on-site renewable energy generation.

HVACR and lighting in building spaces together comprise the majority of energy use and obtaining efficiencies in these two areas can result in a significant amount of cost savings, as well as gains in compliance with the 2030 energy reduction goals. Building automation and energy management systems are designed to tell us how much energy and water we use, how we're consuming our resources, and how well we are managing comfort and safety in the workplace.

## Energy Usage Reporting Requirements

Environmental sustainability and energy performance analysis help organizations monitor and reduce energy consumption and their carbon footprint. With more and more organizations seeking ESS and other building certification, energy performance tools are the latest addition to facility management software systems. Many solutions have monitoring, reporting and forecasting capabilities.

Monitoring tools track how much energy is used in an area of a building, and the amount of greenhouse gas emissions the building produces. Reporting and analytics tools aggregate this information so that facility managers can identify energy consumption trends and make informed business decisions. Forecasting tools help organizations understand the financial impact of energy efficiency that help save energy costs over time.

**Reduce Energy Related Expenses**

Some organizations are taking a look at their energy performance for the first time. Reporting dashboards calculate total energy consumption while helping to identify operational inefficiencies. This kind of analysis demonstrates how an organization is performing and where there's room for improvement, while encouraging sustainable behavior among a building's occupants. Organizations can often see an immediate savings in energy-related costs by implementing environmental performance dashboards that can track no / low / mid / high cost saving opportunities.

# 7 – ENERGY & Buildings Management Software For Facilities

*Credit: ENERGY STAR Portfolio Manager.*

Many energy management software systems are designed to perform in sync with and/or are a component of facility and property management software systems. Most facility and property management software systems feature the components listed below, but the one we're going to focus on in this chapter is the first one, environmental sustainability & energy performance analysis.

- Environmental sustainability & energy performance analysis.
- Mange assets and track important equipment information.
- Manage maintenance costs.
- Automate maintenance workflows.
- Create and manage recurring tasks.
- Increase asset efficiency.
- Streamline work order processes (e.g., repair requests, completion tracking).
- Reduce space and maintenance costs.

As noted in the previous chapter, the Energy Use Intensity (EUI) metric will be the Key Performance Indicator (KPI) environmental sustainability & energy performance analysis. The one environmental sustainability & energy performance software program that provides the industry standard for energy analysis, tracking and savings is EPA's free ENERGY STAR Portfolio Manager program.

## Other Types of Energy and Facilities Management Software

With more than a hundred vendors in the facilities and property management software landscape, this market can be difficult to navigate but there's no excuse for not using one, preferably one that integrates with EPA's ENERGY STAR Portfolio Manager. Vendors use different terms to describe software functionality for energy management and have varying strengths and weaknesses where energy management is the emphasis. Buyer beware!

Most of the energy management software systems will have Building Automation System (BAS) and/or an Energy Management System (EMS) capabilities. Others are more facilities and property management focused, others more maintenance and operations centric. They are categorized in a handful of functional categories and are known as Computer-Aided Facility Management (CAFM), Computerized Maintenance Management Software (CMMS), Enterprise Asset Management (EAM) and Integrated Workplace Management System (IWMS).

Even Building Information Modeling (BIM) programs now have post design and construction capabilities that can track and manage energy resources. Meanwhile, software is becoming available that will interconnect different facility software systems linking BAS/EMS, IWMS, CMMS/CAFM programs and BIM.

No particular software providers are endorsed here, however, for a list of the leading vendors and the pros and cons of their capabilities, please visit the Appendix at the end of the book for ENERGY and Facilities Management Software Review Providers links for more information.

### BAS/EMS

In this day and age, most properties and facilities should have a Building Automation System (BAS) and/or an Energy Management System (EMS). BAS and EMS software systems provide a single control center that handles the remote monitoring and operation of building systems such as electricity, lighting, plumbing, HVACR and environmental control systems. Continual monitoring of all these systems ensures a reliable working environment for personnel and visitors and is an effective tool for resource conservation and waste minimization.

### CMMS/CAFM

Computerized Maintenance Management System (CMMS) and Computer-Aided Facility Management (CAFM) software packages maintain a database on the maintenance and operations in an organization as well as the facilities and properties. Viewed by some professionals as the nervous system of a facility, CMMS/CAFM packages produce status reports and documents detailing and summarizing maintenance, operations, facility and property activities and statistics.

### EAM

Enterprise Asset Management (EAM) involves the management of the maintenance of physical assets of an organization throughout each asset's lifecycle. EAM is used to plan, optimize, execute, and track the needed maintenance activities with the associated priorities, skills, materials, tools, and information. This covers the design, construction, commissioning, operations, maintenance and decommissioning or replacement of plant, equipment and facilities.

### IWMS

An Integrated Workplace Management System (IWMS) is a software platform used by enterprises which integrates the five key components of functionality into a single technology platform and database repository, or from a storage receptacle. It is an enterprise platform that supports the planning, design, management, utilization and disposal of an organization's location-based assets.

**BIM**

Building Information Modeling (BIM) is a shared 3D digital representation of the physical and functional characteristics of the built environment. It is a knowledge resource for information about a facility, designed to form a reliable basis for management decisions during a facility's life cycle. The basics of BIM revolve around the ability to insert, extract, update or modify information to support and reflect the responsibilities of the facility manager.

## The Many Benefits of Using Facility Management Software (FMS)

The current and post-pandemic facility management challenges are upon us—and for many, the old ways of facility management will have to change with these turbulent times.

FM's and O&M personnel who are not already using a facility management software (FMS) program can improve their operations and bottom line by utilizing a vast choice (over 400) of FMS programs (also known as CAFM and CMMS) geared towards a variety of operations and industries.

Facility management software programs help organizations plan and effectively execute facility management processes and functions such as:

- Asset management.
- Equipment information tracking.
- Recurring task management.
- Work order fulfillment.
- Room scheduling.
- Vendor management.
- Maintenance workflow automation.
- Maintenance cost management.

Facility managers can use facility management software (FMS) to track, plan and manage the operations of their facilities. The systems allow facility managers to be more efficient in carrying out various administrative functions such as ensuring the building is properly inspected, maintained, and repaired.

Depending on where they are used, facility management systems can provide important information about the properties being managed and just as important, these systems support operational and strategic plant management. Advanced FMS systems have intuitive user interfaces and are powered by multiple technologies that utilize cloud storage for O&M team access.

Nearly every industry can benefit from a FMS system including but not limited to maintenance, corporations, small and medium business, oil and gas, schools, churches, utilities, hospitals, construction, hospitality, data centers, retail, self-storage and more.

## What is Facility Management Software (FMS)?

FMS is short for facility management software and its purpose is to help your business operate more efficiently by organizing, planning, tracking, and simplifying your facilities management and maintenance operations.

Facility managers can use FMS, also known as Computer-Aided Facility Management (CAFM) and Computerized Maintenance Management System (CMMS), to track, plan and manage the operations of their facilities, properties, and their various assets.

These software systems that go by various names allow facility and property managers to be more efficient in carrying out various administrative functions such as ensuring the building is properly inspected, maintained, and repaired. Advanced FMS systems have intuitive user interfaces and are powered by multiple technologies that utilize cloud storage for O&M team access.

Depending on where they are used, facility and property management systems can provide important information about the properties and buildings being managed and just as important, these systems support operational and strategic plant management. Here are the most common questions asked about FMS software:

### What is a FMS Used For?

FMS software is extremely versatile and fits the needs of most businesses. It's primarily used by helping you organize, plan, track, and simplify maintenance operations. Improvements are made by facilitating the tracking of work orders, scheduling preventative maintenance, receiving, and handling external work requests, managing assets and part inventories, and generating maintenance reports.

### How Does a FMS Help Work Orders?

Work order management is a task that companies often find to be quite troublesome due to how complicated and unorganized it can be. A proper FMS helps you organize and track your work orders with ease. A FMS allows you to see the work that needs to be done, who is assigned to do it, how much time was spent on it, how many resources were used, which invoices are related to the work, and much more. Also, work orders can be tied to specific assets, giving you valuable data that allows you to make critical, money-saving business decisions, such as if an asset will need to be replaced immediately or if it has more life to it.

### How Does a FMS Help Preventative Maintenance?

The numerous benefits of Preventative Maintenance are very well-known: equipment lasts longer, less energy consumed, fewer production delays, and more. FMS maintenance software creates an easy-to-use platform that enables you to automatically schedule work weeks, months, even years into the future. The work is assigned to the correct person for the job. They're automatically reminded about the upcoming work. You'll be able to track all of the PM in your FMS dashboard, where you'll be able to see how long a job took and see if they're being done on time.

**How Does the Best FMS Help Work Requests?**

Manually handling work request is an incredibly daunting and cumbersome task. A proper FMS software system allows anyone in your organization to submit a work request. The work request is then automatically delivered to the right maintenance worker for the job. Upon completion of the work, the requestor is then automatically notified.

**How Does a FMS Help Track Asset History?**

A FMS system allows you to easily track anything you consider valuable to asset in your organization, including, but not limited to work orders, predictive maintenance, preventative maintenance, labor, and parts cost, and much more. You'll be able to attach important information to each asset, such as manuals, PDFs, serial numbers, and more. Each asset can have its own repository of important information.

**How Does a FMS Help Manage Spare Part inventories?**

In addition to tracking larger things like work orders and Preventative Maintenance, a FMS system helps you keep a running inventory or critical tools and parts for your maintenance operations. These important parts are automatically integrated with Work orders and preventative maintenance. Your technicians will be able to ensure they have the correct parts on hand before performing the work. You'll also have access to detailed reporting that shows how many parts have been used within a period of time, how many you'll need in the upcoming future, and more.

**How Does the Best FMS Help With Reporting?**

The beauty of a FMS is it puts your valuable data to work for you. You'll have access to reporting that you had previously only dreamed about, and some that you didn't even know existed! You'll be able to easily answer questions such as 'is the correct maintenance work being done?,' 'which equipment is costing us the most?,' 'where is our maintenance team spending the majority of their time?,' 'which asset is breaking down the most?,' 'who is our best performing maintenance team member?,' and more! Axxerion FMS reporting empowers you with answers to your questions.

**How Can a FMS Be Installed?**

There are two ways to install a FMS: either as an on-premise solution or as a cloud-based SaaS solution. On-premise solutions are installed on your office's existing servers, maintained by your IT staff, and often incur large setup and ongoing costs. Cloud-based FMS solutions are more popular because they are setup on Axxerion's server systems. You won't have to worry about configuring servers or dealing with performing server maintenance. Axxerion offer advanced storage and security features, including frequent data backups so you'll never lose your valuable data.

**How Long Does a FMS Implementation Take?**

There are many factors to consider when putting a timetable on a FMS implementation. Some things to consider are how large your business is, how many features and modules you are looking to implement, how is your maintenance and management team going to buy-in to using a new software system and which FMS installation you are going with. At Axxerion, our average customer is set up within minutes, with a full successful implementation taking only a few weeks.

**How Often is FMS Software Updated?**

The frequency of FMS software updates depends on the type of installation that you choose. Cloud-based FMS software is updated quite frequently, often daily. On-premise FMS installations is typically updated by your IT team between once a quarter to once per year.

**Where is the FMS Data Stored?**

FMS data storage is dependent on the type of installation that you choose. If you go with the cloud-based FMS option, then your data is stored securely on Axxerion's servers. Your data is backed up frequently so you can rest assured that it will never be lost. If you go with an on-premise FMS installation, then your data is stored on the server at your location.

**What Industries Benefit From a FMS System?**

Nearly every industry can benefit from a FMS system, including Maintenance, Corporations, Small and Medium Business, Oil and Gas, Schools, Churches, Utilities, Hospitals, Construction, Hospitality, Data Centers, Retail, Self-Storage and more.

**Does FMS Software Work for Small Businesses as Well as Large Corporations?**

Yes, FMS software is designed to work well with businesses of all sizes.

# 8 – ENERGY Surveys, Inspections, Audits & Commissioning For Facilities

*Credit: RAND Engineering & Architecture, DPC*

The SMART concept can be applied to energy surveys, inspections, audits and commissioning. SMART is an acronym for Specific, Measurable, Assignable, Realistic and Time-related. It's widely used in business environments to define plans, strategies, and specially, objectives to achieve them—such as energy savings.

This chapter will cover the Specific part and the first SMART concept for energy assessments. The ENERGY STAR Portfolio Manager and the other types of energy and facilities management software can provide the Measurable, Assignable, Realistic and Time-related and those four concepts will be as unique to each property, facility and organization as are each facility/property manager and CFO unique compared to each other.

Many CFO's and facility/property managers assume they're using SMART goals in their efficiency plans. Sadly, this may not be the case. If they haven't developed and implemented a Sustainable Energy Buildings Plan (SEBP) and are not utilizing the best energy and building management software systems available, the chances are they're not reducing energy usage to its full potential.

The only way to find out, with a variety of options, is to perform energy surveys, inspections, audits and/or commissioning. Some buildings may require a simple survey, some more defined site inspections, others an in-depth energy audit, and still others a retro or recommissioning of their highest energy consuming equipment or system.

## Conducting Energy Assessments

ENERGY STAR partners have found that conducting plant assessments is vital to a strong energy management program, for without them, it's difficult to continuously improve energy efficiency and demonstrate savings.

Energy assessments can be conducted by internal staff, external energy service professionals, or a combination of both. As previously noted, they can be simple survey, some more defined site inspections, others an in-depth energy audit, and still others a retro or recommissioning of their highest energy consuming equipment.

Regardless of the type of assessment, it's recommended that the team represent varied expertise, including process engineers, maintenance experts, systems managers, energy specialists, etc. if these resources are available. If they aren't, energy consultants and independent contractors can assist.

Plant assessments vary in their focus and depth of involvement based on the program needs and resources available to energy managers. Most organizations can perform surveys and inspections with their own staff, while most will rely on energy consultants and independent contractors to perform the audits and commissioning.

**Energy Treasure Hunts**

An Energy Treasure Hunt is a form of assessment that engages employees to identify low cost or no cost energy saving opportunities by focusing on improving the day-to-day operations of existing equipment. Unlike traditional energy assessments that typically rely on outside experts, a two to three-day Energy Treasure Hunt engages internal cross functional staff to find the opportunities.

By using internal resources, the Energy Treasure Hunt process helps build energy teams and internal processes for managing energy with a focus on continuous improvement. The advantage of starting with an in-house energy survey is that it focuses on improvements that often can be made immediately and without significant expenditures.

**Exploring Ways to Save – Non-Business Hours**

After the facility tour, teams should begin to look for energy efficiency opportunities in their respective areas. If the Energy Treasure Hunt begins on a non-operational day, the teams should focus on investigating savings opportunities that can only be found when the facility is not carrying out its typical operations. Teams might look for:

- Lights, computers, and other equipment that has been left on.

- HVACR systems that have been left running or HVACR operations beyond standard temperature set points.

- Lighting that is too bright, not efficient, or not directed to necessary tasks.

- Air compressors operating when not needed or system air leaks.

- Other building or process equipment left running unnecessarily.

**Exploring Ways to Save – Business Hours**

Energy Treasure Hunt teams can focus on energy efficiency opportunities that are observable during regular operations and in typical equipment processes. These might include:

- Temperature set point too high or too low.

- Compressed air being wasted.

- Energy supply equipment, such as compressed air and lights, not interlocked to turn off at the same time as production equipment.

- Production equipment operating but no product being produced.

During staff lunch and break periods, teams should check the facility for equipment that could be turned off, such as:

- Workspace lighting, motors, and pumps that are not in constant use.

- Equipment that does not have a lengthy start time but is left on.

## Energy Audits Using ASHRAE Levels 1, 2 & 3

An energy audit is the key to a systematic approach to decision-making in the area of energy management. The primary function of an energy audit is to identify all of the energy streams in a facility in order to balance total energy input with energy use. The four main objectives of an energy audit are as follows:

- To establish an energy consumption baseline.

- To quantify energy usage according to its discrete functions.

- To benchmark with similar facilities under similar weather conditions.

- To identify existing energy cost reduction opportunities.

Before beginning an energy audit for a building or portfolio of buildings, a preliminary energy use analysis must be carried out. This analysis requires access to energy and natural gas consumption and cost data for the last 24-36 months. The purpose of this analysis is to compare the Energy Usage Index (EUI) of each building with the national average and to identify both high and low energy performers. Once the analysis is completed a recommendation is made as to which buildings should be audited first and the type of audits to be carried out.

Energy audits vary in depth, depending on the potential at a specific site for energy and cost reductions and the project parameters set by the client. As per ASHRAE (American Society of Heating, Refrigerating and Air-Conditioning Engineers) standards there are three types of audits, outlined below.

**ASHRAE Level 1 – Walk-Through Analysis/Preliminary Audit –** The Level 1 audit alternatively is called a simple audit, screening audit or walk-through audit and is the most basic.

**ASHRAE Level 2 – Energy Survey and Analysis** – A Level 2 audit includes the preliminary ASHRAE Level 1 analysis, but also includes more detailed energy calculations and financial analysis of proposed energy efficiency measures.

**ASHRAE Level 3 – Detailed Analysis of Capital Intensive Modifications** – This level of engineering analysis focuses on the potential capital-intensive projects identified in the Level 2 analysis and involves more detailed field data gathering as well as a more rigorous engineering analysis.

Completing an energy audit of a facility provides an organization with customized energy conservation measures and may also indicate energy consuming equipment is not operating at peak performance. If that's the case, retrocommissioning of the existing equipment in question is required.

## Retrocommissioning and Recommissioning

Specifically, retrocommissioning is a form of commissioning. Commissioning is the process of ensuring that systems (lighting, HVACR, etc.) are designed, installed, functionally tested, and capable of being operated and maintained according to the most energy efficient operating criteria.

**Retrocommissioning** is the same systematic process applied to existing buildings that have never been commissioned to ensure that their systems can be operated and maintained according to the most energy efficient operating criteria. For buildings that have already been commissioned or retrocommissioned, it is recommended that the practices of recommissioning or ongoing commissioning be applied.

**Recommissioning** is the term for applying the commissioning process to a building that has been commissioned previously (either during construction or as an existing building); it is normally done every three to five years to maintain top levels of building performance and/or after other stages of the upgrade process to identify new opportunities for improvement. The LEED EB+OM building certification requires recommissioning every 5 years as part of the LEED building recertification process.

In **Ongoing Commissioning**, monitoring equipment is left in place to allow for ongoing diagnostics. Ongoing commissioning is effective when building staff have the time and budget not only to gather and analyze the data but also to implement the solutions that come out of the analysis.

Building owners, managers, staff, and tenants all stand to gain from the retrocommissioning process. It can lower building operating costs by reducing demand, energy consumption, and time spent by management or staff responding to complaints. It can also increase equipment life and improve tenant satisfaction by increasing the comfort and safety of occupants.

Energy researchers statistically analyzed more than 224 new and existing buildings that had been commissioned, totaling over 30 million sf. of commissioned floor space (73% existing buildings and 27% new construction). The results revealed the most common problem areas and showed that both energy and non-energy benefits were achieved. Analysis of commissioning projects for existing buildings showed a median commissioning cost of US$0.27 per sf. energy savings of 15%, and a simple payback period of 0.7 years.

A recent study of retrocommissioning revealed a wide variety of problems—those related to the overall HVACR system were the most common type. Retrocommissioning provided both energy and non-energy benefits—the most common of these, noted in one-third of the buildings surveyed, was the extension of equipment life.

The top candidates for retrocommissioning are those buildings with:

- A low ENERGY STAR performance rating or a high energy use index (Btu per sf., Btu per patient, and so forth) that cannot be explained, or unexplained increases in energy consumption.

- Persistent failure of building equipment, control systems, or both.

- Excessive occupant complaints about temperature, airflow, and comfort.

# 9 – Facilities ENERGY Benchmarking Using Portfolio Manager

*Credit: Strategic Management Insight.*

The EPA currently maintains performance ratings for all major commercial building types, including banks, financial institutions, courthouses, hospitals (acute care and children's), hotels and motels, K–12 schools, medical offices, offices, residence halls and dormitories, retail stores, supermarkets, warehouses (refrigerated and nonrefrigerated), wastewater treatment plants and a limited number of categories of manufacturers.

The benchmarks and ratings for such buildings are made available through the ENERGY STAR Portfolio Manager which allows users to set up private accounts to track building portfolios, set baselines, share information, and document the results of their efforts to improve energy performance. Again, Portfolio Manager is your "go to" energy measurement and savings tool.

This rating system is based on statistically representative models that compare the energy consumption of a building to similar buildings from a national survey conducted by the United States Department of Energy (DOE) every four years called the Commercial Building Energy Consumption Survey (CBECS). Essential information from this survey can highlight facility performance criteria such as:

- **Energy Use** – Shows rating, EUI, source EUI and change from baseline.

- **Environmental** – Shows rating, EUI, change from baseline energy use, and change from GHG emissions.

- **GHG Emissions** – Shows EUI, current GHG emissions, baseline GHG emissions, and change from baseline.

- **Water Use** – Shows water use, water cost, wastewater use, and wastewater cost.

- **Financial** – Shows annual cost of energy, water, and cost/SF of energy and water.

A score of 50 indicates that the building, from an energy consumption standpoint, performs better than 50% of all similar buildings nationwide, while a score of 75 indicates that the building performs better than 75% of all similar buildings nationwide. Ultimately, EPA expresses the rating on a 1-100 scale where 1 point on the scale represents 1 percentile of the commercial building market.

To track and manage energy performance, each building's rating is expressed on a scale of 1 to 100, which denotes the percentile of performance relative to the other buildings in the national CBECS data set. A rating of 75 means a particular building outperforms approximately 75 percent of its peers; these buildings are in the top quartile for their building type and are eligible to earn an ENERGY STAR label.

## The Department of Energy's (DOE) ENERGY STAR Portfolio Manager

The ENERGY STAR Portfolio Manager is free and focused on energy management and cost savings. It also tracks water and waste management that are not covered in this book. It is also the essential energy management software program required to provide the necessary energy performance and benchmarking information for most of the US based green building certification programs such as LEED that are covered in Chapter 14 - ENERGY Certifications for Facilities and Managers. No facility should be without it!

ENERGY STAR's Portfolio Manager can assist in evaluating and tracking a facility's energy consumption, help identify underperforming facilities, generate an ENERGY STAR score, track energy savings from implementation of energy efficient measures, and evaluate potential energy saving measures for a facility. With the assistance of ENERGY STAR Measurement and Tracking Tool: Portfolio Manager, facility owners and managers can make more informed decisions on topics and matters that are based on the energy performance of their facility.

By entering basic information about a facility and its energy consumption data, the tool calculates annual energy consumption, which can be compared to other similar facilities using the CBECS benchmarking data. Some facilities that meet certain criteria can take this further and use the tool to benchmark energy usage against facilities across the nation and determine the building's ENERGY STAR score.

You've heard it before you can't manage what you don't measure. That's why EPA created ENERGY STAR Portfolio Manager®, an online tool you can use to measure and track energy and water consumption, as well as greenhouse gas emissions. Use it to benchmark the performance of one building or a whole portfolio of buildings, all in a secure online environment. Benchmark any type of building.

You can use Portfolio Manager to manage the energy and water use of any building. All you need are your energy and utility bills and some basic information about your building to get started. Are you designing a new commercial building, or remodeling, or adding an addition to an existing one? You can also use Portfolio Manager to set your energy use target and see how your estimated design energy stacks up against similar existing buildings nationwide.

## Using ENERGY STAR Portfolio Manager to Benchmark EUI

In general, buildings with lower ratings have a greater opportunity to improve their energy performance levels. The areas with the greatest energy savings potential throughout most building types are typically lighting, HVACR systems, and other high energy usage items such as refrigeration, office and kitchen equipment.

Organizations and businesses are reducing their energy use by 30 percent or more through effective energy management practices that involve assessing energy performance, setting energy savings goals, and regularly evaluating progress. Building-level energy performance benchmarking is an integral part of this effort. It provides the reference points necessary for developing sound energy management practices and strategies and for gauging their effectiveness.

ENERGY STAR's Portfolio Manager can assist in evaluating and tracking a facility's energy consumption, help identify underperforming facilities, generate an ENERGY STAR score, track energy savings from implementation of energy efficient measures, and evaluate potential energy saving measures for a facility. With the assistance of ENERGY STAR Measurement and Tracking Tool: Portfolio Manager, facility owners and managers can make more informed decisions on topics and matters that are based on the energy performance of their facility.

Do buildings that consistently benchmark energy performance save energy? The answer is yes, based on the large number of buildings using the U.S. Environmental Protection Agency's (EPA's) ENERGY STAR Portfolio Manager to track and manage energy use. Over 35,000 buildings entered complete energy data in Portfolio Manager and received ENERGY STAR scores for 2008 through 2011, which represents three years of change from a 2008 baseline.

These buildings realized savings every year, as measured by average weather-normalized energy use intensity and the ENERGY STAR score, which accounts for business activity. Their average annual savings is 2.4%, with a total savings of 7.0% and score increase of 6 points over the period of analysis.

## Setting Up a Facility for an ENERGY STAR Score

After registering as a Portfolio Manager user, the next step is to create a facility in Portfolio Manager and populate the necessary data with the following:

- Essential building information such as year built, building type, floor area, number of occupants, etc.

- Break out space uses that are fundamentally different from the defined core building space.

- Twelve (12) months of monthly energy consumption data.

Facilities can be grouped in Portfolio Manager to show how certain groups of facilities may be performing against an entire portfolio or within the group.

**Internal Benchmarking** allows an organization to compare the energy use at a building or group of buildings to that of others in that organization. The results can be used within an organization to compare energy performance among buildings, to identify buildings with the greatest potential for improvement, to track performance over time, to identify best practices at individual sites that can be replicated, and to increase management's understanding of how to analyze and interpret energy data.

In **External Benchmarking,** buildings are compared to other, similar buildings. The results can be used to assess performance relative to peers in the same sector or industry and across other sectors and industries, to compare the energy performance of facilities against a national performance rating, to track performance against industry or sector performance levels, to identify new best practices for improving building performance, to increase understanding of how to analyze and evaluate energy performance, and to identify high-performing buildings for recognition opportunities such as the ENERGY STAR label.

## Setting and Interpreting Energy Performance Goals

The next step is to set goals and targets for improving energy efficiency. Portfolio Manager has features that allow the user to set energy performance goals and estimate how much energy will need to be saved to meet those goals. This feature allows reasonable goals and targets to be set for the facility and provides an estimate of how much energy must be saved to achieve the goals.

Energy savings can be tracked as energy conservation measures are implemented. The impact of past energy-saving measures as a whole across the entire facility can also be estimated. Once energy performance improvements have been implemented, you can evaluate how much energy these improvements have saved. If energy performance improvements have been implemented in the past, Portfolio Manager can also help in evaluating the savings received from these improvements as a whole or over a period of time.

Based on the scope of the project, benchmarking can be repeated over time to assess progress relative to the defined goals and to encourage continuous improvement. It is important to track progress and compare actual energy consumption data with stated goals. This comparison will show whether or not goals have been achieved and how much money energy savings have contributed to the organization's bottom line. The comparison will also help to identify the organization's best practices and will inform decisions about how to achieve future goals. Setting new goals on a regular basis will help foster an environment of continuous improvement.

## Develop a Benchmarking Plan and Data Requirements

Facility managers can use benchmarking data to screen their portfolio of facilities or properties. The information will help them decide where to do on-site audits, identify which sites would get the best return from tune-ups and retrofits, or even just know when to remind local managers about energy-efficient behaviors. With this data, they can also calculate what is needed to meet an internal or external goal across the organization.

The quantities of electricity, natural gas, steam, chilled water, and other delivered energy sources may be gathered at the corporate, campus, building, process, or equipment level. These data may come from accounting systems or bill-handling services. Depending on the types of energy used, more-detailed consumption data may be available from process or equipment submeters. All energy sources must be accounted for a minimum of one year to develop a rating score.

A successful benchmarking study often requires the help of other parties, who should be identified and engaged at the beginning of the process. Primary candidates for participation include departments or organizations that own the data that are needed for the benchmarking effort. For external benchmarking, look for partners in the same industry or sector. An effective partnership requires that the partners understand the objectives, expected outcomes, and schedule of the project, and know their role and the costs and benefits of their participation.

By using the tracking tools, continuously collecting information about the facility and setting new energy performance targets, sustainability goals can be achieved and met. Consultants with industry expertise and relevant training such as the LEED AP Operations & Maintenance, Facility Management Professional (FMP), and the Certified Construction Manager (CCM) credentials can provide ENERGYSTAR Portfolio Manager set-up, monitoring, and benchmarking services in lieu of performing them in-house.

## What Is Your Building's ENERGY STAR Score?

The Environmental Protection Agency's EPA's 1 - 100 ENERGY STAR score is an external benchmark for assessing the performance of commercial buildings.

The ENERGY STAR score, expressed as a number on a simple 1 - 100 scale, rates performance on a percentile basis: buildings with a score of 50 perform better than 50% of their peers; buildings earning a score of 75 or higher are in the top quartile of energy performance.

First introduced in 1999, the score has been adopted by leading organizations across the United States because it offers a simple way to evaluate measured energy use, prioritize investments, and communicate relative performance across a portfolio of buildings.

Recognizing the widespread adoption of the ENERGY STAR score in the commercial marketplace, EPA continually reviews and updates the technical approach to ensure accurate, equitable, and statistically robust scores. The overall objectives of the ENERGY STAR score are to:

- Evaluate energy performance for the whole building.

- Reflect actual metered energy consumption.

- Equitably account for different energy sources.

- Normalize for building activity.

- Provide a peer group comparison.

Once developed, the ENERGY STAR score is programmed into EPA's online measurement and tracking tool, ENERGY STAR Portfolio Manager®. The following steps are used to compute the score for an individual property:

- Enter data into Portfolio Manager.

- Compute actual source energy use intensity.

- Compute the predicted source energy use intensity.

- Compute an efficiency ratio comparing the actual use with the predicted use.

- Assign a score based on how the ratio compares with the national distribution.

**Facility Management Objectives**

EPA has identified the following objectives for a successful energy performance metric in California facilities:

1. Evaluate energy performance for the whole building. Rather than examining specific pieces of equipment within a building, a whole building metric accounts for the interactions among the various system components. For example, a particular HVAC system may be designed with efficient components, but if it is over-sized relative to the actual heating and cooling loads it will not perform efficiently. A robust analysis must account for the energy use of the whole building.

2. Reflect actual metered energy use. The ENERGY STAR score must reflect the actual metered or billed energy consumption at a property. It cannot be based on predicted or simulated energy use, as simulations often fail to account for both the impact of building operation and maintenance patterns and the interactions among building systems.

3. Equitably account for different energy sources. Source energy accounts for both energy consumed at the site as well as energy used in generation and transmission. This approach is the most equitable for assessing properties with different fuel mixes and buildings with onsite power generation systems. In addition, source energy is more reflective of energy costs and GHG emissions.

4. Normalize for building activity. The intent of the ENERGY STAR score is to provide a fair assessment of energy performance, taking into account operational conditions required for the business activities within the building. Normalization requires adjustments to account for factors such as weather, operating hours, and the number of workers.

5. Provide a peer group comparison. A peer group comparison enables building owners and operators to track not only their improvement over time, but also how they stack up when compared to others with the same primary business function (e.g., retail store).

## Computing Your Score

To receive an ENERGY STAR score in Portfolio Manager, you must enter 12 full calendar months of energy data for all energy types, in addition to complete data on property use details such as hours of operation and workers. To determine the score, Portfolio Manager will compute both the actual source **energy use intensity (EUI)** and the predicted source EUI based on these inputs. The ratio of actual source EUI to predicted source EUI is the efficiency ratio, which can be mapped through a lookup table to determine the 1 - 100 ENERGY STAR score. A score of 75 indicates that the building performs better than 75% of its peers.

Ultimately, the purpose of this guide is to show facility managers how the ENERGY STAR Measurement and Tracking Tool: Portfolio Manager can assist in evaluating and tracking a facility's energy consumption, help identify underperforming facilities, generate an ENERGY STAR score, track energy savings from implementation of energy efficient measures, and evaluate potential energy saving measures for a facility. With the assistance of ENERGY STAR Measurement and Tracking Tool: Portfolio Manager, facility owners and property managers can make more informed decisions on topics and matters that are based on energy performance.

# 10 – ENERGY Efficient Lighting For Facilities

*Credit: Wildcat Electric Supply.*

Lighting uses about 18 percent of the electricity generated in the U.S., and another 4 to 5 percent goes to remove the waste heat generated by those lights. Lighting in commercial buildings accounts for close to 71 percent of overall lighting electricity use in the U.S.

Lighting consumes close to 35 percent of the electricity used in commercial buildings in the United States and affects other building systems through its electrical requirements and the waste heat that it produces. Upgrading lighting systems with efficient light sources, fixtures, and controls can reduce lighting energy use, improve the visual environment, and affect the sizing of HVACR and electrical systems.

Low, mid and high cost energy saving solutions for electrical systems were covered briefly in Chapter 5 – Potential Energy Cost Savings For Facilities. However, when initial investment, life-cycle costing, and energy savings are taken into consideration for electrical equipment upgrades, the end of this chapter provides a detailed list of these with the greatest energy savings potential.

## A Whole-System Approach

Many lighting-efficiency efforts are oriented toward the installation of specific pieces of equipment, such as electronic ballasts or compact fluorescent downlights. But as with many other types of complex systems, the interactions among system elements in lighting equipment create energy and power savings that can be greater than the sum of their parts.

Starting with a system of fixtures containing four energy saver T12 lamps, an upgrade to standard T8 lamps and electronic ballasts can produce energy savings of more than 25 percent; using high-performance T8 lamps boosts savings to more than 40 percent.

The next option begins to capture some system interactions. Each fixture is equipped with a specular reflector and a new acrylic flat prismatic lens. Because these are significantly better at getting light out of the fixture than the old, white-painted luminaire and aged diffuser, the fixture can be delamped by 50 percent—to two high-performance T8 lamps—and still provide virtually the same amount of light for the task. Adding reflectors and new lenses to the fixtures enables delamping—a reduction in the number of lamps required per fixture—with little loss in light levels, for a savings of 71 percent compared to the base case.

Adding occupancy sensors and daylighting controls can boost savings to more than 80 percent compared to the base case, and more than 50 percent compared to a system with standard-grade T8 lamps and electronic ballasts.

## Use Efficient Light Sources

Efficient lighting begins with the use of as much daylight as possible. After that, choose the lamp / ballast / fixture combination that will maximize efficiency while balancing the considerations of lighting quality and quantity described above. There is a wide variety of light sources to choose from including fluorescent (linear and compact), high-intensity discharge (HID), and newer sources such as induction lamps and light-emitting diodes (LEDs).

These sources vary widely in their efficacy, color quality, service life, and the applications for which they are best suited. Historically, fluorescent lighting has been used for high-quality, general purpose indoor diffuse lighting. HID lighting has been used for industrial and outside lighting.

However, technical advances and a flood of new products have led to some crossover in the way these lamps are applied—fluorescent lighting is now the most effective choice for many industrial and exterior lighting applications, while HID lighting (specifically metal halide) is now a good choice for some interior uses.

Fluorescent lighting systems offer high efficacy, long life, and good light quality, and they generally have few operational limitations for most indoor lighting applications. They are the best choice for general lighting in commercial, institutional, and industrial spaces with low to medium ceiling height. In addition, the introduction of high-intensity fluorescent lamps and fixtures makes fluorescent systems a leading choice for areas with high ceilings (more than 15 feet)—the type of application that used to be the exclusive domain of HID light sources (see sidebar).

### Picking the Right Fluorescent Lamp

Manufacturers have introduced a wide array of linear fluorescent lamp choices, including reduced-wattage, premium, and high-performance versions. There are also choices of CCT, CRI, lamp diameter, light output level (standard, high-output, or very high output), and starting method (rapid-start, programmed rapid-start, or instant start). For most general lighting upgrades, the best choices are:

- T8 (eight-eighths of an inch in diameter).
- Four-foot lamps.

Standard-output lamps are more efficient and less costly than high output (HO) and very high output (VHO) systems, and they are available with a wider range of color temperatures. T5HO lamps are often used for high-bay applications because their high-intensity light is useful in large spaces.

- CRI in the 80s.
- CCT of 3,500 K to 4,100 K.

Ballast choices can be equally bewildering. The best choices for ballasts are:

- Electronic (high-frequency) .
- Instant-start.
- Programmed-start.
- Universal-input.

Finally, make sure that lamps and ballasts are compatible. Most lamps are only compatible with one starting method; the major exception is high-performance T8s, which can use either rapid or instant-start ballasts.

### Compact Fluorescent Lamps (CFL)

Use compact fluorescent lamps (CFLs) to replace incandescent lamps in downlights, sconces, table lamps, task lights, and wall washers. They cost more initially than incandescent lamps do, but quickly pay for themselves through energy and maintenance savings. The longer the annual operating hours, the more attractive the economics of CFLs become, because more incandescent relamping costs are being avoided per year.

One of the most common uses of CFLs in commercial buildings is in recessed downlight cans. A wide range of fixtures is now available for this fixture class, some with very good reflector designs, good optical control, and dimming capabilities. Care must be taken in this application to ensure that excess heat buildup does not shorten the lamp life.

When using CFLs, remember these key points:

- Go for a 3:1 ratio.
- Limit the number of CFL types.
- Use dedicated fixtures.
- Choose CFLs that have earned the ENERGY STAR rating.

## Other Light Types

Depending on the area of usage and purpose, some of these other lighting choices might be a better choice in your facility.

**High-Intensity Discharge (HID) Lamps –** Wherever an intense point source of light is required, HID light sources are the primary alternative to high-wattage incandescent lamps. Although HID lamps can provide high efficacy in a wide range of sizes, they have special requirements for start-up time, restrike time, safety, and mounting position.

**Metal Halide Lamps –** Metal halide lamps offer good color quality and efficacies of up to 100 lm/W. Were it not for several limitations of the older probe-start technology, metal halide lamps might be considered the ideal light source.

**Sodium Lamps –** There are two types of sodium lamps: high-pressure sodium (HPS) and low-pressure sodium (LPS). HPS lamps, which produce a yellowish light, vary widely in their efficacy and color quality.

**LED's (Light Emitting Diodes) –** LED's are the latest and most exciting technological advancement in the lighting industry and are small, solid light bulbs which are extremely energy efficient and long lasting.

**Induction Lamps –** Also called electrodeless lamps, consist of a high-frequency power generator, a coupling device that generates a magnetic field (essentially an antenna), and a glass housing that contains the gases and phosphor coating—no electrodes required.

## Submetering & Current Transformer (CT) Monitoring

You can't manage what you can't measure. Electric submeters can be installed at discrete points in a building to monitor energy usage by one or more electrical loads (e.g., individual HVACR units) and/or one or more segments of a building. Electrical submeters connect to individual circuits using Current Transformers (CTs).

Every entity that has an energy saving interest in a building (e.g., building owners and operators, energy service companies, consultants, engineering firms, etc.) will want real-time submetering data to track utility costs per floor, per tenant, per equipment, etc. Submetering and CT Monitoring provide a base foundation of understanding consumption profiles in a building.

## Achievable Electrical Energy Targets for Commercial Buildings

Application of specific energy savings measures across all building types and climate zones resulted in cutting energy use by nearly half, according to results of approved research funded by ASHRAE. The national weighted change is 47.8 percent more energy efficient than ASHRAE Standard 90.1-2013 based on site energy and 47.8 percent more energy efficient than ASHRAE standard 90.1-2013 based source on energy.

The question of "how energy efficient can commercial and multifamily buildings become in the near future if first cost is not considered" was explored in ASHRAE 1651-Research Project, "Development of Maximum Technically Achievable Energy Targets for Commercial Buildings: Ultra-Low Energy Use Building Set."

From the resulting list of almost 400 measures, 30 were chosen for additional analysis. Sixteen prototype buildings that were consistent with Standard 90.1-2013, Energy Efficiency Standard for Buildings Except Low-Rise Residential, across 17 climate zones were used as baseline models. The 30 measures were then individually modeled. Each of the 30 measures, often with many options, were applied to each building and climate combination. In general, the measures were applied in the following order:

- Reduce internal loads.

- Reduce building envelope loads.
- Reduce HVACR distribution system losses.
- Decrease HVACR equipment energy consumption.
- Major HVACR reconfigurations.

After each measure was applied to each of the 272 building and climate combinations, if the energy consumption was reduced, it remained in the model. After all, 30 measures (which included 9 electrical and 21 HVACR) were applied, the projected U.S. national weighted energy consumption for new buildings was nearly cut in half compared to Standard 90.1-2013.

The 2 general and 9 electrical energy efficiency measures modeled were:

- Optimal Roof Insulation Level.
- Optimal Choice of Vertical Fenestration.
- LED Exterior Lighting.
- Highest Efficiency Office Equipment.
- High Performance Lighting (LED).
- Shift from General to Task Illumination.
- Optimal Daylighting Control.
- External Light Shelves.
- Daylighting Control by Fixture.

# 11 – ENERGY Efficient HVACR Systems For Facilities

*Credit: Sander Mechanical Service.*

HVACR systems function in a critical role in any building (the "R" is added for refrigeration). Everyone becomes acutely aware of HVACR performance when malfunctions occur. The level of interest has only increased today. Whether concerns about energy efficiency, building sustainability, operations and maintenance, or indoor air quality (IAQ), more visibility is required.

There are many different types of energy efficient HVACR equipment such as package units, split systems, central plants, chillers, boilers, refrigeration, and so on. Each has its own unique energy savings opportunities. However, there are two other options for substantial energy savings, and they are utilizing an energy management systems (EMS) and consistent and certified HVACR maintenance. These last two options use existing HVACR equipment and employ properly trained and/or certified maintenance technicians without any need for any major capital and/or labor expenditures.

When that happens, HVACR systems on average will use at least 15 to 20 percent less energy than those systems maintained by unqualified and uncertified service technicians and facilities and properties management who are not effectively managing their HVACR systems with an EMS system. Of course, all HVACR equipment and systems will deteriorate over time, more quickly without proper and consistent maintenance, so the most efficient energy saving equipment and systems will be the last and most expensive options to consider.

Low, mid and high cost energy saving solutions for HVACR systems were covered briefly in Chapter 5 – Potential Energy Cost Savings For Facilities. However, when initial investment, life-cycle costing, and energy savings are taken into consideration for HVACR equipment upgrades, the end of this chapter provides a detailed list of equipment with the greatest energy savings potential. Before we get there, let's first review the cost savings benefits of using an energy management system (EMS) and then the HVACR quality of installation and maintenance challenge options.

## Benefits of Using an Energy Management System (EMS)

All facility and property managers should be engaged to one degree or another in a Sustainable Energy Buildings Plan (SEBP) that seeks out low cost savings opportunities that are available through optimizing energy management systems. Too often, more emphasis is focused on installing efficient equipment and not enough on managing and operating equipment in an efficient way, such as using an Energy Management System (EMS) which for most organizations is a no cost if existing, to a low-cost opportunity if it needs to be purchased, installed and operated.

A simple definition of an EMS is a system that controls and monitors energy consuming devices, which may include heating and cooling equipment, fans, pumps, dampers, and lighting. Many EMSs can also be used to control refrigeration equipment, industrial processes, or other energy consuming systems. With an EMS in place that is effectively managed, monitored and controlled some simple rules to follow for energy savings are:

- **Using equipment only when needed** – Enforcing this policy often delivers greater energy savings at a lower cost. Lights and HVAC equipment can often be on when they don't need to be; when no one's in the building, or no one is in a particular area of a building. The easiest way to save energy is to turn equipment off when not using it.

- **Use only as much energy as necessary** – It's not uncommon to see light levels that are unnecessarily high, base temperatures that are too warm in the winter or too cool in the summer or more fresh air provided to a space than is necessary. You can choose set points that just the right amount of light or space conditioning that's provided to the building.

The latest energy management systems use Direct Digital Control (DDC). DDC systems can use proprietary software, or they can utilize open protocol standards that allow components from different systems to work together. The building operators can use an EMS for different purposes, but it's primary purpose is generally to ensure occupant comfort and indoor air quality. Beyond that, systems can be used to operate when needed or necessary, thereby maximizing energy savings.

Energy management systems have evolved in complexity over time and are also be known as Building Management Systems (BMS), or Building Automation Systems (BAS), or Energy Management Control (EMC) systems. The most basic form of energy management consists of a simple time clock and thermostat and these systems are still the best choice of control in certain buildings today. In larger buildings and more complicated systems, there's usually a computer that provides a user interface that pulls all the information together for the building operator.

Generally, an EMS consists of three essential elements:

- Sensors that measure things like temperature, pressure, and light levels, which are used to initiate responses by the system.

- Controllers that compare a signal received from a censor to a desired set point and set out a signal to a control device for action.

- And the controlled devices which are the equipment that receives the signals from the controllers, such as a fan, a pump, a damper, light switch, etc.

## The HVACR Quality Installation/Maintenance Challenge

Using California as a prime example, commercial buildings there consume more electricity than any other sector in California, constituting 38 percent of the state's power use and over 25 percent of natural gas consumption. To meet the state's Zero Net Energy mandates AB 758 is a significant challenge, with Heating, Ventilation, Air Conditioning and Refrigeration (HVACR) as a major source of potential energy savings.

The California Long-Range Energy Efficiency Strategic Plan states that quality installation and maintenance should become the industry and market norm (CPUC 2008). More specifically, this goal states that 100% of HVACR systems would be installed to quality standards and optimally maintained throughout their useful life by 2020, with HVACR related permits obtained for 50 percent of installations by 2015 and 90 percent or more by 2020 (CPUC 2008). This would reduce overall energy use and lower energy costs.

Pressures on California's HVACR workforce are high, as a very large percentage of the state's 58,000 incumbent workers are not trained in energy efficiency, and many of those trained have difficulty keeping up with changes in technology, codes, and standards.

Poor installation and maintenance of residential and commercial HVACR systems is a widespread problem. The California Energy Commission (CEC) estimates that up to 50% of new HVACR systems and up to 85% of replacement systems are not installed and maintained to a quality level of specification. Given the high potential savings associated with improving residential and commercial installation and maintenance practices, the CPUC set targets to improve HVACR performance by 50% by 2020 and 75% by 2030.

The HVACR industry has struggled to provide qualified technicians, and market conditions rarely value quality installation and maintenance (QI/QM). Less than 10 percent of HVACR systems obtain legally required pre-installation local building permits and 30-50 percent of new central air conditioning systems are not being properly installed. As a result, Californians pay a large price for the lack of quality installation and maintenance, with commensurate poor performance. The factors that have led to a 20-30 percent increase in the peak energy needed to provide consumers with the cooling and comfort they demand on hot summer afternoons has been accompanied by an estimated 30 percent increase in carbon emissions.

## HVACR Training, Certifications and Credentials

Requirements for HVACR certification will vary by type of certification and by organization offering it. For example, for some certifications, students might need to have a completed course of training while for others, time on the job provides the sufficient knowledge needed to pass an exam. Additionally, different types of testing may be required for certifying exams, varying from a written test to a hands-on display of skills. Here is a look at some common certifying organizations and their certifications:

## EPA Section 608 Certification

As mentioned above, the EPA requires those who work with refrigerants or refrigeration systems to seek an EPA Section 608 certification. The EPA certifications that are available include: Type I for small appliances; Type II for high-pressure appliances; Type III for low-pressure appliances; and Universal, which is a comprehensive credential. A plurality of organizations provides coursework, preparation materials, and exam sites to test for these certifications.

## North American Technician Excellence (NATE)

NATE offers a wide range of specialty certifications at varying levels. NATE requires that aspiring HVACR technicians pass a core exam and one specialty exam in order to achieve certification. The specialty exams are divided into three categories: installation, service, and senior.

- **Installation Specialties:** The five installation specialties include air conditioning, air distribution, heat pump (air-to-air), oil heating (air), and gas heating (air).

- **Service Specialties:** The nine service specialties – with many offered in Spanish – include air conditioning, air distribution, oil heating (air), gas heating (air), heat pump (air-to-air), hydronics gas, hydronics oil, commercial refrigeration, and light commercial refrigeration.

- **Senior Level Technician Certification:** The senior level technician certification is open to candidates with two NATE specialty certifications.

NATE also offers the **Industry Competency Exams (ICE)**—formerly called the ARI/GAMA competency exams—covering a range of residential and commercial HVACR systems and related skills.

## HVAC Excellence Programs

HVAC Excellence offers a number of certifications for both high school students who have completed vocational training and for more advanced HVAC technicians. By setting program standards and verifying that they have been met, trainees and technicians can meet the challenges facing the HVACR quality control and assurance requirements by continuous improvement in a way that prepares applicants for energy efficient and compliant services. To accomplish this, HVAC Excellence provides the following programs:

**Student Outcome Assessments for High Schools** – Secondary (high school) HVACR instructors need to validate if a student has the retained knowledge to move on to the next level, or if they need additional training. HVAC Excellence offers the tools needed to accomplish this through our Heating, Electrical, & Air Conditioning Technology (H.E.A.T.) and H.E.A.T. + student outcome assessments.

**Employment Ready Certifications** – Post-Secondary (college, trade school, apprenticeship, manufacturers, wholesaler) instructors need to validate if a student has the retained knowledge necessary for employment in the HVACR industry, or if they need additional training. HVAC Excellence offers the tools needed to accomplish this through their Employment Ready Certifications.

**Technician Certifications: Professional Level** – HVAC Excellence offers progressive levels of certification that identify an individual's knowledge and skill level through each phase of their career. Professional Level Technician Certifications covering a variety of HVACR components are intended for experienced technicians, is a series of discipline-specific, closed-book, comprehensive written exams, that were specifically designed for technicians with two or more years of field experience.

**Master Specialist: Hands-On** – The HVACR industry and consumers have greatly benefited from technician certification. It has been accepted as a tool to validate that a technician has the retained knowledge of heating and cooling systems. However, no one can be sure if a technician could properly apply this knowledge, unless they are Master Specialist Certified.

### Refrigeration Service Engineers Society (RSES)

The RSES provides several different levels and subject areas of HVACR certification including the mandatory EPA Section 608 Certification for refrigeration workers mentioned above. There are eight specialized written examinations: commercial air conditioning, commercial refrigeration, controls, domestic service, dynamic compression, heating, heat pump, and HVAC-R electrical. Please note that these specialized credentials are exclusively for active members of RSES. The organization also provides R-410A training and certification.

## Achievable HVACR Energy Targets for Commercial Buildings

As previously noted, the application of specific energy savings measures across all building types and climate zones resulted in cutting energy use by nearly half, according to results of approved research funded by ASHRAE. The national weighted change is 47.8 percent more energy efficient than ASHRAE Standard 90.1-2013 based on site energy and 47.8 percent more energy efficient than ASHRAE standard 90.1-2013 based source on energy.

The question of "how energy efficient can commercial and multifamily buildings become in the near future if first cost is not considered" was explored in ASHRAE 1651-Research Project, "Development of Maximum Technically Achievable Energy Targets for Commercial Buildings: Ultra-Low Energy Use Building Set."

"The value of establishing such ultra-low-energy targets for buildings is two-fold," Jason Glazer, principal engineer for GARD Analytics who oversaw the project, said. "These targets will indicate to building design professionals what may be achieved if first cost is not considered and challenge the creativity of those professionals to achieve similar results in actual designs with the real-world constraints of first costs. They also will help advance design guides, standards and codes by providing an ultimate goal."

For the project, researchers assembled a list of energy efficiency measures that can be included in the design of non-residential buildings. The list included both commonly used and cutting-edge energy efficiency measures, according to Glazer.

From the resulting list of almost 400 measures, 30 were chosen for additional analysis. Sixteen prototype buildings that were consistent with ASHRAE Standard 90.1-2013, Energy Efficiency Standard for Buildings Except Low-Rise Residential, across 17 climate zones were used as baseline models. The 30 measures were then individually modeled. Each of the 30 measures, often with many options, were applied to each building and climate combination. In general, the measures were applied in the following order:

- Reduce internal loads.
- Reduce building envelope loads.
- Reduce HVACR distribution system losses.
- Decrease HVACR equipment energy consumption.
- Major HVACR reconfigurations.

After each measure was applied to each of the 272 building and climate combinations, if the energy consumption was reduced, it remained in the model. After all, 30 measures (which included 2 general, 7 electrical and 21 HVACR) were applied, the projected U.S. national weighted energy consumption for new buildings was nearly cut in half compared to Standard 90.1-2013.

The 21 HVACR energy efficiency measures modeled were:

- High Performance Fans.
- High Performance Ducts to Reduce Static Pressure.
- Demand Controlled Ventilation/CO2 Controls.
- Multiple-Zone VAV System Ventilation Optimization.
- Optimal Water/Air Cooling Coils.
- Occupant Sensors for Air Handling Equipment.
- Energy Recovery Ventilators.
- Indirect Evaporative Cooling.
- High Efficiency/Variable Speed Packaged DX Cooling.
- High Efficiency Heat Pumps.
- Ground Source Heat Pump.
- High Efficiency and Variable Speed Chillers.
- Heat Recovery from Chillers.
- High Efficiency Boilers.
- High Efficiency Building Transformers.
- Chilled/Cooled Beam.
- Dedicated Outside Air System with Heat Recovery.
- Underfloor Air Distribution.
- Hybrid/Mixed Mode Ventilation.
- Radiant Heating and Cooling and DOAS.
- Variable Refrigerant Flow Air Conditioning.

# 12 – California's Time-of-Use ENERGY Rate Changes For Facilities

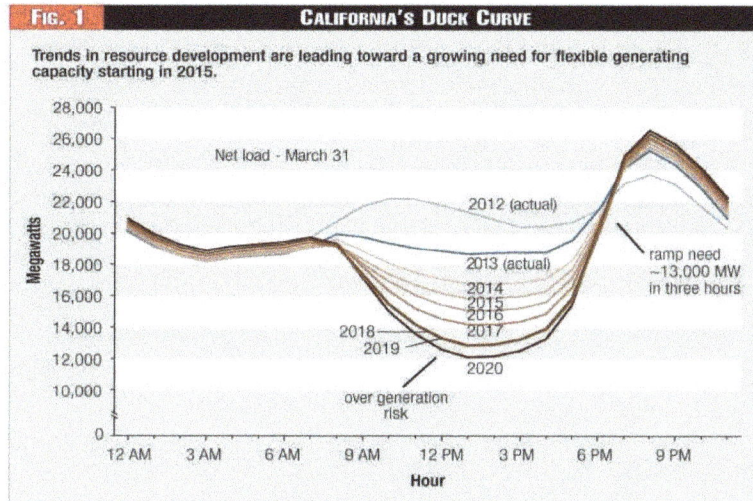

**FIG. 1** — **CALIFORNIA'S DUCK CURVE**

Trends in resource development are leading toward a growing need for flexible generating capacity starting in 2015.

*Credit: Credit: Energy Institute at Haas.*

Because of solar power's success, utilities across the country are adopting pricing policies that place an increasing emphasis on time-variable rates and demand charges. For an average commercial energy user today, 60% of energy spent is based not on how much energy you use, but when you use it.

In California, for example, utilities have changed the timing and price of Time-of-Use (TOU) rates in a way that diminishes solar project economics unless developers pair solar with energy storage. In addition, utilities have also increased demand charges by more than 100% across the last decade.

That means businesses are getting charged more for their peak energy usage each month. If those peaks occur when time-based rates are highest, it can mean a huge energy bill, and can impact the savings from solar energy. Solar energy alone does not address the most expensive demand peaks, which now with the new rate structures, often occur in the late afternoon when solar production drops. By employing both solar and energy storage systems (ESS), businesses can reduce not only energy charges, but also address demand peaks that may occur when solar output goes down.

Solar will continue to expand but with the shift in energy demand to non-PV producing time frames in the evening when demand peaks, the newest and most promising renewable is the use of ESS and the DER technology that allows them to flatten end user energy usage as well as distribute surplus energy back to the grid all the while reducing buildings energy costs and improving an organizations bottom line.

Be it financial and/or environmental, it's the best of both worlds as the following statistics show:

- U.S. energy storage deployment nearly doubled in 2018 as the nation installed 350.5 MW, 777 MWh—over 80% more than was deployed in 2017 in terms of megawatt-hours, according to a new report.

- Behind-the-Meter (BTM) storage accounted for 53% of the total deployment in megawatts while front-of-the-meter (FTM) installations accounted for 47%, according to the U.S. Energy Storage Monitor 2018 Year-in-Review. FTM installations often had durations of four hours or more.

- Report authors from Wood Mackenzie and the Energy Storage Association expect the energy storage market to double in 2019, deploying 1,681 MWh. By 2024, they expect annual deployments to exceed 4.4 GW that are powered by DERs.

For California's buildings, a larger percentage (now 60% as of 2020) of the state's energy is supplied by renewable resources and of those renewal resources solar power is by far the largest. That's the good news!

As the transmission of energy moves from these sources to power substations, electrical energy is distributed to fill the various power needs of California's buildings. During that process between 61% - 86% of the generated power is lost, wasted, along the way and this power supply is also imbalanced, creating power surges and sparking electrical fires. The bad news!

In addition, utilities have also increased demand charges by more than 100% over the last decade. The ugly news!

**What is the California Public Utilities Commission (CPUC) Doing About This?**

California's Public Safety Power Shutoff (PSPS) incidences are becoming more prevalent, and back-up and energy storage power sources are more critical than ever. This includes black start systems that can restore a buildings back-up energy power system without relying on the external electric power transmission network to recover from a total or partial shutdown.

California's utilities have long scheduled their peak hours rate, known as time of use (TOU) rates—from around 11 am to about 6 pm. These hours are when solar generation is at its highest, enabling large energy users to rely on their on-site solar power and avoid exposure to several hours of high on-peak rates.

However, the rise of solar power generation—both Behind-the-Meter (BTM) and at the utility scale—has disrupted the dynamics of the supply mix supporting California's electric grid. This disruption is known as the Duck Curve and utilities are adapting by shifting the 5 hour on-peak demand period to 4 pm-9 pm with changes to their TOU rate schedules.

**How do These TOU Rates and Peak Time Changes Affect My Building's Energy Needs?**

The Duck Curve creates several challenges for utilities. The first is accommodating the late afternoon spike in demand. This often requires a reliance on natural gas peaker plants, which can generate power quickly but are expensive to operate on a regular basis.

Compounding the cost and supply problem is the sudden energy surge needed in the early evening that overwhelms the electrical grid, causing electricals surges, power outages, and fires up and down the state of California. Business are suffering from higher costs, unreliable demand, and mandatory power outages.

## What's Your Energy Usage? Good? Bad? Or Ugly?

For utilities, electricity is generally more expensive and complex to deliver when demand is high. To help cover these costs, California's utilities have traditionally imposed Time-of-Use (TOU) rates, which created a daily schedule that applies different prices for power based on demand trends on the grid. When demand is highest, prices are highest under TOU rates.

In the past, daily grid demand ramped up in the morning, peaked from noon into the early afternoon as temperatures and air conditioning usage increased, and then gradually decreased as the day progressed. Though there is some additional nuance to the scheduling, California's utilities have long scheduled on-peak hours—during which rates were the highest—from around 11 am to about 6 pm. Off-peak hours, meanwhile, were generally applied through the other hours of the day.

For utilities, TOU rates helped increase revenue to cover the high costs of delivering power when demand was high. For energy consumers, this created an incentive to minimize reliance on the grid for power during on-peak hours. This has long been a significant part of the value of on-site solar photovoltaics (PV) for the state's large energy consumers. The hours when solar generation is at its highest levels happen to coincide with the on-peak hours, enabling large energy users to rely on their on-site solar power and avoid exposure to several hours of high on-peak rates every day.

However, the rise of solar power generation in the state—both Behind-the-Meter (BTM) and at the utility scale—has disrupted the dynamics of the supply mix supporting California's electric grid. Utilities are adapting to these new realities with changes to their TOU rate schedules, which will have a significant impact on the business case for behind-the-meter solar PV and Energy Storage Systems (ESS).

## California's Utilities Respond to the 'Duck Curve

From 2007 to 2017, utility-scale solar power generation in California grew from 557 GWh to 24,353 GWh, according to the US Energy Information Administration (EIA). This rapid increase has created a number of serious challenges for the state's utilities, which rely largely on natural gas generation to supply the majority of power on the grid.

Solar production increases in the late morning hours and peaks around noon before tailing off in the late afternoon and early evening. This reduces demand for natural gas during the midday hours, when utilities traditionally imposed higher, on-peak TOU rates. Then, as solar power generation diminishes in the late afternoon hours, utilities face a spike in demand for power from natural gas.

California's Independent System Operator (CAISO) illustrated this trend in the graph below, which is now commonly known as the "duck curve."

The Duck Curve creates several challenges for utilities. The first is accommodating the late-afternoon spike in demand. This often requires a reliance on natural gas peaker plants, which can generate power quickly but are expensive to operate on a regular basis. Compounding the cost problem is that much of this early evening spike in demand falls outside of the traditional on-peak hours when utilities could expect to make up the high cost of delivering power.

In addition to the high costs, the reduction in midday demand has depressed a traditional source of revenue for natural gas generators, while high levels of solar production have decreased electricity prices, sometimes leading to negative prices. For utilities, TOU rates helped increase revenue to cover the high costs of delivering power when demand was high.

In response, California's utilities have begun adjusting their TOU rate schedules to account for the duck curve. San Diego Gas & Electric (SDG&E) shifted on-peak hours for its summer season to 4 pm-9 pm, from its previous schedule of 11 am-6 pm. Pacific Gas & Electric (PG&E) and Southern California Edison (SCE) implemented the same types of schedules for on-peak hours in 2019.

Under these new schedules, the utilities apply on-peak rates when demand for natural gas spikes in the late afternoon to early evening hours, helping them adapt to the economic realities of the duck curve. For the state's large energy consumers, meanwhile, the shift disrupts the economics of behind-the-meter solar PV and energy storage.

## The Impact of New TOU Rate Schedules on Solar PV and Energy Storage

Under the new TOU rate schedules, peak production for a solar PV system will occur largely during the new off-peak hours at midday. This undercuts the value of stand-alone solar PV as a source for off-grid power to avoid on-peak rates.

To illustrate the impact of the shift in TOU rates on a stand-alone solar PV system, analyzed was a 2-MW solar PV system installed at an office building with $1.2 million in annual energy spend, 7 GWh of annual energy usage, and a peak load of 1.6 MW. The latest TOU rate schedules reduce the value of the solar PV system by 19% over a 20-year period!

However, combining solar PV with energy storage can enable large energy users to use their self-generated power more strategically. If customers can charge an Energy Storage System (ESS) with their on-site solar PV assets during off-peak hours, they can transition their facility onto that low-cost energy during on-peak hours. Distributed energy resources (DER) optimization software facilitates this process, charging the ESS with power generated via solar PV and automatically transitioning the facility's load onto the on-site capacity available to reduce consumption from the grid when on-peak rates are applied.

Looking at the same building analyzed above, adding a 500 kW/1 MWh ESS with the existing on-site solar PV actually makes up the value that the system would have lost as a result of the new

TOU rate schedules. That equates to a difference of about $1.9 million.

The shift in TOU rate schedules will also affect the business case for stand-alone energy storage. Again, DER optimization software plays an important role in managing these costs, automatically charging the batteries at times when power prices are lowest and deploying the power during on-peak hours.

To understand the impact on energy storage, calculated was the value of a 630 kW/1 MWh stand-alone ESS for a food-processing facility with annual energy spend of about $650,000, annual usage of 3 GWh, and a peak load of 1 MW. For this facility, the new TOU rate schedules would increase the value of an ESS by 16%, resulting in more than $3.1 million in total value over a 20-year period.

## Looking Ahead: The Long-Term Value of Energy Storage in California

The change in TOU rate schedules came as a result of a fundamental shift to a more renewable-heavy power generation mix. As the fundamental market dynamics behind the electric grid evolve, energy storage and distributed energy resources (DERs) will become increasingly important to help large energy users adapt to these market realities and brace for the impact.

For example, the rise of electric vehicles (EVs) in California threatens to disrupt the grid. In 2017, EV sales in California reached nearly 95,000, up 28.5% from the year prior and considerably higher than the next closest state, New York, which saw just over 10,000 in sales of EVs in 2017, according to data from the Alliance of Auto Manufacturers and IHS Markit. Large energy users in California could see multiple challenges as a result of the rise of EVs.

- **Grid-level challenges:** How will the rise of EV charging affect the grid? What new challenges will energy providers face, and how will those challenges affect energy consumers?

- **Facility-level challenges:** As EV charging becomes a necessity to integrate on-site—whether to charge a fleet of EVs owned and operated by the company or to provide an amenity to customers, tenants, or employees—how will the equipment affect the facility's load profile and energy costs?

Energy storage and DERs position customers need to adapt to these kinds of new developments seamlessly. The ability to store and deploy power on-site, whether generated via on-site resources or sourced at times when grid costs are at their lowest, enables energy users to manage their reliance on the grid strategically. TOU rates are an important part of the equation, but they are far from the only way California's energy consumers can create value by maximizing their flexibility with DERs.

Additionally, the gradual decrease in incentives for DERs in California makes it important for those in California who would benefit from DERs to act soon. The Self-Generation Incentive Program (SGIP) offered by California's Public Utilities Commission (CPUC) will diminish over time, leaving less incentive capital available as more customers take advantage of the program in the next few years. Additionally, the investment tax credits for DERs are set to decrease from

30% in 2018 to 10% by 2021.

## How Time-of-Use (TOU) Rate Changes Affect Your Electric Bill

The utilities and several major environmental groups see time-of-use rates as a valuable tool to help clean up the state's power supply. California has a growing abundance of cheap solar power during the middle of the day, so much that utilities sometimes have been forced to pay other states to take it. But the sun goes down every evening just as people get home from work, forcing utilities to fire up expensive, polluting gas plants.

Time-varying rates are meant to encourage homes and businesses to shift their power use away from high-demand periods, when energy is dirtier and more expensive, and toward low-demand periods when energy is cleaner and less expensive. For California's three largest public utility companies SDG&E, SCE and PG&E pictured above, their "on-peak" time-of-use periods are now between 4 p.m. to 9 p.m., when energy costs are 60% more during summer weekdays.

### Why Are There Peak and Off-Peak Hours?

Under a TOU rate, customers pay different prices per kilowatt hour (kWh) of electricity that they use, depending on when they use it. Pricing varies by time of day and can also vary based on the day of the week (weekend or weekday) and the time of year. TOU rates are characterized by different prices between "peak hours" and "off-peak" hours, and the exact details of a customer's TOU rate will depend on the specific rate plan offered by their electric utility.

Electricity costs more during certain designated "peak hours" for customers on a time of use rate plan. These hours are typically selected to coincide with the times when the demand for electricity is greatest (often in the late afternoon/early evening and the summertime). Solar is abundant during the middle of the day, when people are using the least amount of energy, but it's effectiveness drops off as the sun goes down and power usage goes up.

### The Economics and Future of Time-of-Use Electricity Usage

One reason for peak pricing is because utilities must have additional energy generation resources available to meet the needs of the grid during limited times when energy demand is highest. By pricing electricity higher during times that typically have the highest demand, TOU rates are intended to provide price signals that encourage customers to shift their energy usage to other periods.

Time-variable rate programs are already offered on a voluntary basis in nearly every state. Although participation in voluntary TOU programs has been low to date, as many states consider efforts to modernize the electrical grid and reduce peak energy consumption, TOU rates (and other related time-based rate structures) may become increasingly prevalent. There are multiple approaches that utilities take when it comes to time-varying energy costs, but TOU rates are one of the most common.

# 13 – ENERGY Code Compliance Measures For Facilities

*Credit: CEC.*

As the leader in the nation on environmental stewardship, energy reduction, sustainability, and green building standards, California has set an ambitious goal in accomplishing these objectives starting with Assembly Bill 32: California Global Warming Solutions Act of 2006. From this progressive legislation, California has developed and approved the CALGreen Code, Zero Net Energy and Assembly Bills 758, 802, 2514 and 2868 as well as Senate Bill 350 requirements.

AB 32 requires California to reduce its GHG emissions to 1990 levels by 2020—a reduction of approximately 15 % below emissions expected under a "business as usual" scenario. When Gov. Brown took over, he and the California Energy Commission (CEC) had a much bigger ambition to set Zero Net Energy (ZNE) goals above and beyond AB 32 requirements by reducing GHG emissions for all new and existing commercial buildings to 40 % below 1990 levels by the year 2030.

## Zero Net Energy (ZNE) Standards and Challenges

In 2008 the California Public Utility Commission (CPUC) issued its Zero Net Energy (ZNE) goals for all new residential construction by 2020 and for commercial buildings by 2030. California's Zero Net Energy (ZNE) Standard is already in place through the state's energy and green building standards codes (Title 24 Parts 6 & 11) to achieve the 2020 and 2030 ZNE construction targets. The 2013 Energy Code will reach 70% of the residential ZNE goal, the 2016 Energy Code 85% and the 2019 Energy Code will meet the 100% goal of ZNE. By 2030 every new school is supposed to be a zero net energy building.

A Zero-Energy Building, also known as a Zero Net Energy (ZNE) building, Net-Zero Energy Building (NZEB), or Net Zero Building, is a building with zero net energy consumption, meaning the total amount of energy used by the building on an annual basis is roughly equal to the amount of renewable energy created on the site. These buildings still produce greenhouse gases because on cloudy (or non-windy) days, at night when the sun isn't shining, and on short winter days, therefore, conventional grid power is still the main energy source.

Because of this, most zero net energy buildings still get half or more of their energy from the grid. Buildings that produce a surplus of energy over the year may be called "energy-plus buildings" and buildings that consume slightly more energy than they produce are called "near-zero energy buildings" or "ultra-low energy houses".

To help attain these ZNE measures, California requires their existing buildings to be energy efficient. To ensure attainment of these goals, CALGreen building code requirements were adopted by the California Building Commission (CBC), and included in modified Part 11, of the Title 24 building code.

To summarize the California Energy Efficiency Strategic Plan, the state has ambitious goals for the development of zero net energy buildings. These include:

- All new residential construction will be zero net energy (ZNE) by 2020.

- All new commercial construction will be ZNE by 2030.

- 50% of commercial buildings will be retrofit to ZNE by 2030.

- 50% of new major renovations of state buildings will be ZNE by 2025.

- AB 32 – The Global Warming Solutions Act.

- AB 758 – Comprehensive Energy Efficiency in Existing Buildings Law.

- AB 802 – Mandatory Energy Benchmarking & Disclosure.

- SB 350 – Clean Energy & Pollution Reduction Act.

- AB 2514 – Energy Storage.

The CPUC released a draft Commercial Zero Net Energy Action Plan (Commercial ZNE Plan) in December 2017. A prior Commercial ZNE Plan was finalized in June 2011, but the updated plan will align with changes to the market and state policies such as better integration of distributed energy resources into the grid and a decline in the cost of solar generation and energy storage.

The new Commercial ZNE Plan will add zero net energy for "multi-building projects, campuses and large-scale developments." The new draft also looks at how existing buildings can attain zero net energy use. California also has a goal that 50 percent of all existing commercial structures will achieve zero net energy use by 2030.

## AB 758 – Comprehensive Energy Efficiency in Existing Buildings Law

California has implemented a groundbreaking law, AB 758 that requires all existing buildings that fall significantly below Title 24 to improve their efficiency. This first-of-its-kind legislation has the potential to dramatically reduce the amount of energy and electricity that buildings consume and could be a model for the rest of the country. More than half of California's 13 million residential buildings and over 40% of commercial structures were built before the implementation of Title 24 in 1978. According to the California Energy Commission's (CEC) "cost effective" estimates, the new law could reduce projected electricity use by 9% and projected natural gas use by 6% in California, which translates to $4.5 billion dollars in consumer savings.

AB 758 requires the California Energy Commission (CEC) to develop and implement a comprehensive program to achieve cost-effective energy savings in the state's existing residential and nonresidential building stock that fall significantly below the efficiency required by the current version of Title 24. The law also requires the California Public Utilities Commission (CPUC) to investigate the ability of each electrical and gas corporation to provide various energy efficiency financing options to their customers for the purposes of implementing the program.

Change is inevitable and planning for AB 758 as early as possible is the first step in successfully managing it. Seeking assistance, at a minimal cost, from a qualified consultant to perform a sustainable facilities assessment and develop an action plan for meeting AB 758 requirements can save energy costs, prevent lost opportunities, and avoid future aggravation. An assessment and action plan can also create high performance building operations and sustainable systems that allow facility and property managers to do more with less and be the enablers of their own success.

## California's Green Building Code

The purpose of the California Green Building Code (CALGreen for short), Part 11 of Title 24, is to improve public health, safety and general welfare by enhancing the design and construction of buildings through the use of building concepts having a reduced or negative impact on energy usage or a positive environmental impact that encourages sustainable construction practices for most all building types.

Among the new requirements under CALGreen, every new building in California will have to reduce water consumption by 20%, divert 50% of construction waste from landfills and install low VOC materials. Separate indoor and outdoor water meters for non-residential buildings and moisture-sensing irrigation systems for large landscape projects will be required. There will be mandatory inspections of energy systems, such as furnaces and air conditioners for non-residential buildings over 10,000 square feet. According to the California Air Resources Board (CARB), the mandatory provisions will reduce greenhouse gas emissions by 3,000,000 metric tons by 2020.

Although CALGreen was initially developed for new construction, lackluster new building starts in the Great Recession economy blunted the code's influence. To fix this problem a new section of Chapter 5, Division 5.7 – Additions & Alteration to Existing Non-Residential Buildings was added, and now widens the 2019 CALGreen's focus to include existing buildings. Regarding school construction, CALGreen is required for any new campus that's built and entire campuses that are rebuilt.

The trigger for existing buildings is when a project has a minimum of 1,000 sf. of construction and a minimum cost of $200,000 for remodels, additions and alterations. Only buildings above those levels have to meet CALGreen Code requirements. The City of Los Angeles led this effort to include existing commercial buildings in their local amendments to the 2010 CALGreen Code because approximately 90% of the impact for green construction is going to be realized in existing buildings through remodels, additions and alterations.

## AB 802 – Mandatory Energy Benchmarking & Disclosure

In October 2015, the State of California passed AB 802 (that replaced existing Energy Use Disclosure Law AB 1103 effective January 1, 2016) to provide building owners access to their building energy use data from utilities, and to track consumption in their buildings. The purpose of AB 802 is to help building owners, tenants, and others better understand the energy consumption of their buildings through standardized energy use metrics.

Under the new program, a utility must maintain energy usage data for all buildings served by that utility for at least the most recent 12 complete calendar months. A utility would need to provide the benchmark data to a building owner or operator within four weeks of a request. In addition, AB 802 requires the CEC to develop regulations to govern the delivery of benchmark data to the CEC and the public disclosure of such data.

For building owners and managers, there are five important data points when reviewing and understanding AB 802:

- Non-residential and multi-family buildings over 50,000 sq. ft. (with certain exceptions).

- Multi-family buildings over 50,000 sq. ft. and with 17 or more dwelling units.

- Owners must report their ENERGY STAR score to the California Energy Commission every two years.

- The initial reporting period for non-residential building was June 1, 2018. After that, fines can be levied as noted below.

- The first reporting period for multi-family starts April 1, 2019 with data due by June 1, 2019. After that, fines can be levied as noted below.

## Energy Reporting (And Use) Law Enforcement in California

If you have not benchmarked your building in California yet, you'll need to do so quickly. The challenges owners and operators may be facing include:

**Fines:** According to the bill's Section 1685 Violations, penalties for non-compliance include, "A Civil penalty to be $500-$2,000 per day for each category of data the person did not provide and for each day the violation has existed and continues to exist." In this case, a "category of data" typically means each energy type and/or meter. The Energy Commission will provide the owner a 30-day grace period to report once notified of a violation.

**Obtaining the Data:** Obtaining consumption data can be a very difficult and tedious process, especially if there are multiple meters and/or tenants within a building. If the meter data is unavailable from a tenant, you'll need to contact your local utility provider for that information. The utility provider is required by law to provide the data, but there is no guarantee when and in what format you will receive it. This can cause delays in reporting, so to avoid missing any critical deadlines, collecting utility data should be your top priority.

**Finding Time to Report**: Several hours are required to fulfill the reporting requirement. This includes identifying all buildings that qualify for energy benchmarking, identifying all meters, and entering all the data and meter information accurately.

**Falling Below Standards:** What if your building falls below the national benchmarking standard? If this is the case, you're likely wasting money through excessive energy consumption.

Even if your building falls below the ENERGY STAR score of 75 (75th percentile of like kind buildings across the nation, and the baseline minimum set by the State of California), you're still in compliance with the bill just for having reported your utility data.

However, owners/operators in buildings that fall below the 75th percentile of their peer group will receive information and resources from the State on how to improve energy profiles. If you learn your building is unnecessarily costing you money, you'll want to assess the best approach of reducing those identified expenses.

**Newly Designed/Constructed Buildings:** These are generally aligned towards State compliance. Buildings that are in design and construction may receive favorable energy reports when utilizing state approved compliance software. However, these simulations do not accurately reflect hours of operation and occupant behavior.

## SB 350 – Clean Energy & Pollution Reduction Act

Lastly, California approved SB 350: Clean Energy & Pollution Reduction Act approved in 2015 that requires the state to double statewide energy efficiency savings in electricity and natural gas end uses by 2030 and create a building energy-use benchmarking and disclosure program. SB 350 is considered the most significant climate and clean energy legislation since the passage of AB 32: California Global Warming Solutions Act that set the statewide goal of reducing greenhouse gas emissions to 1990 levels by 2020.

In addition, AB 32 directed and authorized various state agencies to engage in actions necessary to achieve this goal. Building off of AB 32, SB 350 established California's 2030 greenhouse gas reduction target of 40 % below 1990 levels. To achieve this goal, SB 350 sets ambitious 2030 targets for energy efficiency and renewable electricity, among other actions aimed at reducing greenhouse gas emissions. SB 350 will greatly enhance the state's ability to meet its long-term climate goal of reducing greenhouse gas emissions to 80 % below 1990 levels by 2050.

## AB 2514 – Energy Storage

Assembly Bill (AB) 2514 is California's landmark legislation that will create a smarter, cleaner electric grid, increase the use of renewable energy, save Californians money by avoiding costly new power plants, and reduce greenhouse gas emissions and other harmful air pollutants through the use of energy storage technologies by utility companies.

The 2012 bill requires the California Public Utilities Commission (CPUC) to open proceedings to establish Investor Owned Utility (IOU) procurement targets for viable and cost-effective Energy Storage Systems (ESS) to be achieved by December 31, 2015, and an additional target to be achieved by December 31, 2020. A Publicly Owned Utility (POU) would have comparable requirements and would be required to develop plans to maximize shifting of electricity use for air-conditioning and refrigeration from peak demand periods to off peak periods.

## City / County / Municipal Energy Efficiency Ordinances and Regulations

As building efficiency improvements become more affordable, they are also becoming law. California cities such as Los Angeles, San Francisco, San Diego, San Jose and Berkeley have all enacted ordinances requiring commercial and multi-family buildings to report their annual energy usage. Many states have also implemented state-wide programs, such as California's AB 802, that require energy disclosure and audit reports to be completed.

The Los Angeles Department of Building Safety (LADBS) has released a notice regarding the Existing Buildings Energy and Water Efficiency Ordinance (EBEWE). The purpose of this ordinance is to reduce energy and water consumption in existing buildings in the City of Los Angeles. The ordinance requires existing commercial and multi-family buildings to be benchmarked, audited, retrofitted, and/or retro-commissioned. These efficiency improvements will lower the use of energy, water and greenhouse gas emissions citywide.

Benchmarking through Energy Star's Portfolio Manager software is required for both city- and state-wide legislature, and the Energy Star score reveals big opportunities for energy savings. Benchmarking is becoming common practice not only in the law, but also in making financial and business decisions. Many states and cities are in the process of implementing programs and the great majority of them rely upon EPA's Portfolio Manager to assess operating performance.

For your city's particular ordinances and energy reporting requirements, please visit the Appendix at Existing Building Energy and Water Efficiency Ordinance (EBEWE) Update.

# 14 – ENERGY Certifications For Facilities and Managers

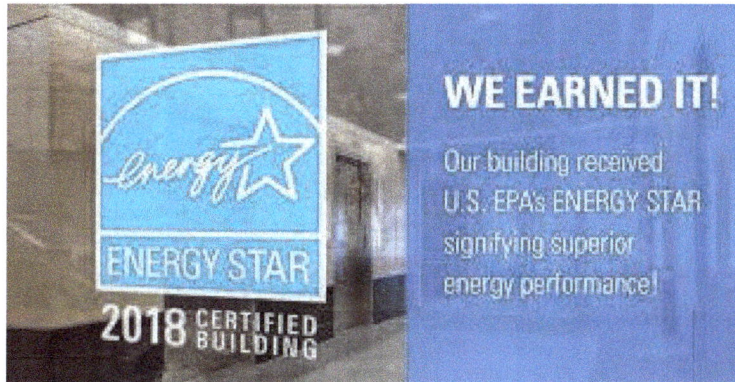

*Credit: ENERGY STAR.*

There are a number of energy efficient building rating systems that have more similarities than differences. While there is no legal or clearly articulated definition of what a "green building" is, these organizations offer standards for green buildings, albeit in slightly different ways.

The other green building standards you may want to consider in addition to the ENERGY STAR Building Certification are LEED, Green Globes, Living Building Challenge, WELL Building Standard, Passive House, Net Zero Energy Building, BOMA 360 Performance Program, CHPS and others.

In terms of LEED alternatives, a growing number of state and local governments are adopting different green building standards that aren't tied to LEED, such as California's statewide CALGreen building code that took effect last year. In addition, several other rating systems are cropping up and gaining momentum, such as the Green Building Initiative's Green Globes, which is touted as a simpler and less expensive rating system.

In addition, some governments are adopting building codes that apply green standards outside of the LEED blueprint. CALGreen represented the first statewide green building code in California, and it eschews outside (third-party) evaluations like LEED's. Listed below are these credentials, by organizations, in alphabetical order.

## American Hospital Association (AHA)

The AHA is the national organization that represents and serves all types of hospitals, health care networks, and their patients and communities.

- **Certified Healthcare Facility Manager (CHCM)** – Is a health care administrator who has passed the prestigious CHFM exam through the American Hospital Association (AHA).

## Association for Facilities Engineering (AFE)

The AFE is a professional membership organization serving all professionals working in the built environment. AFE defines the term-built environment as the surroundings people construct to provide settings for human activity and interaction, ranging in scale from buildings to parks, often including their supporting infrastructure such as water supply and energy networks.

- **Certified Plant Engineer** (**CPE**) – Designed to validate your skills as an experienced facilities engineer who possesses the expertise and the technical knowledge required to successfully ensure the optimal performance of any facility, including project and maintenance/equipment engineering.

- **Certified Professional Maintenance Manager (CPMM)** – Designed to validate your skills as an experienced facilities professional who possesses the basic technical and management expertise and knowledge required to successfully lead a maintenance organization in reducing costs while increasing operating efficiencies through designing and implementing effective maintenance programs utilizing the latest methodologies.

- **Certified Professional Supervisor (CPS)** – Designed to validate your skills as a competent facility team supervisor who possesses the required professional demeanor and expertise to be a leader among other facilities management professionals, capable of motivating and training front-line maintenance technicians to specialized engineers; and to rise above your peers in the necessary elements of administrative, organizational and technical tasks to move to the head of the line for job advancement.

## Association of Energy Engineers® (AEE®)

The AEE® is a nonprofit professional society of over 18,000 members in more than 100 countries. The mission of AEE is to promote the scientific and educational interests of those engaged in the energy industry and to foster action for Sustainable Development. AEE offers the following certifications:

- **Certified Energy Manager (CEM)**
- **Energy Manager in Training (EMIT)**
- **Certified Energy Auditor (CEA)**
- **Certified Energy Auditor – Master's Level (CEAM)**
- **Certified Measurement & Verification Professional (CMVP)**
- **Certified Business Energy Professional (BEP)**
- **Certified Building Energy Simulation Analyst (BESA)**
- **Certified Building Commissioning Professional (CBCP)**
- **Certified Building Commissioning Professional – Master' Level (CBCPM)**
- **Certified Energy Procurement Professional (CEP)**
- **Certified Geo-Exchange Designer (CGD))**
- **Certified Lighting Efficiency Professional (CLEP)**
- **Certified Power Quality Professional (CPQ)**
- **Certified Carbon Reduction Manager (CRM)**

- **Certified Carbon Auditor Professional (CAP)**
- **Certified in the Use of RET Screen (CRU)**
- **Certified Sustainable Development Professional (CSDP)**
- **Distributed Generation Certified Professional (DGCP)**
- **Existing Building Commissioning Professional (EBCP)**
- **High Performance Building Professional (HPB)**
- **Green Building Engineer (GBE)**
- **Certified Residential Energy Auditor (REA)**
- **Renewable Energy Professional (REP)**
- **Energy Efficiency Practitioner (EEP)**
- **Certified Performance Contracting & Funding Professional (PCF)**
- **Government Operator of High Performance Buildings (GOHP)**
- **Certified Demand-Side Management Professional (CDSM)**
- **Certified Indoor Air Quality Professional (CIAQP)**
- **Certified Industrial Energy Professional (CIEP)**
- **Certified Water Efficiency Professional (CWEP)**

## Association of Physical Plant Administrators (APPA)

APPA represents more than 18,000 educational facilities professionals from over 1,300 learning institutions worldwide. APPA's community represents the broadest coalition of educational facilities professionals possible, ensuring a diversity of experiences and situations, and availability of best practices.

- **Certified Educational Facilities Professional (CEFP**) - Is a certification designed for both aspiring and existing educational facilities professionals with eight years of combined education and professional facilities management experience. Earning the CEFP demonstrates that you have a mastery of professional expertise and is a mark of superior proficiency in the core competencies for education facilities professionals.

- **Pathway to Professionalism (P2P)** – A new program designed to help educational facilities organizations and their institutions keep pace with accelerating rate of change, while providing continuous learning opportunities for their staffs and schools.

## Building Owners and Managers Institute (BOMI) International

BOMI International is the educational arm of the Building Owners and Managers Association (BOMA). All certificate programs provide the fundamental knowledge you need to better understand your job responsibilities and are a good way to begin your journey toward earning a BOMI International designation. A certificate that fits your needs is listed below:

- **BOMA 360 Performance Program** – The program is sponsored by Building Owners and Managers Association (BOMA) International. The BOMA 360 Performance Program, intended to be an overarching evaluation of building operations, recognizes buildings that meet industry best practices in building operations and management, safety and risk management, training and education, energy performance, environment and sustainability, and tenant/community relations.

- **Property Administrator Certificate (PAC)** —Ideal for those who manage the overall operations of a building or a portfolio of buildings.

- **Property Management Financial Proficiency Certificate (PMFP**) —Ideal for those responsible for analyzing, managing, and investing in real estate assets.

- **Facilities Management Certificate (FMC)** —Ideal for those who manage the ongoing operation and maintenance of facilities.

- **Building Systems Maintenance Certificate (SMC**) —Ideal for those who operate and maintain multiple building systems.

- **Building Energy Certificate (BEC)** —Ideal for those in operational and system maintenance roles.

- **Certified Manager of Commercial Properties™ (CMCP™)** —Ideal for those looking to take the first step in building a successful career in commercial real estate.

## Collaborative for High Performance Schools (CHPS)

**CHPS Verified™** and **CHPS Verified Leader™** will ensure that a school project is well-designed, operated, and maintained K-12 educational facilities that enhance student performance; positively impact student, teacher, and staff health and wellness; make education more enjoyable and rewarding; and promote positive environmental stewardship.

The following facility and property management related credentials in some way or form help their users, and ultimately their facilities and properties, to become more efficient, economical and/or sustainable. As part of that process, energy management and cost savings are an integral part of their success and contribute to energy savings and efficiency. The most popular and recognized credential and certification programs are from the following organizations.

## ENERGY STAR Building Certification

ENERY STAR was originally developed by the U.S. Environmental Protection Agency (EPA) as a voluntary labeling program to promote energy-efficient products and reduce greenhouse gas emissions. In the late 1990s, EPA partnered with the U.S. Department of Energy (DOE) to increase the scope of the ENERGY STAR program by launching a whole building program, ENERGY STAR for Buildings.

**ENERGY STAR for Buildings** includes specifications for Existing Buildings, Commercial New Construction, Industrial Energy Management, and ENERGY STAR for Small Business. The program includes three tools as follows for assisting and encouraging organizations in their efforts to reduce energy use and limit resulting greenhouse gas emissions:

- **ENERGY STAR Portfolio Manager –** This software tool allows organizations to measure, track, and compare their energy use to other buildings. It is the backbone of the ENERGY STAR for Buildings program and a key verification component of the LEED for Existing Buildings: Operations & Maintenance rating system.

- **ENERGY STAR Task Manager** – This no-cost online tool allows architects and building owners to set energy targets and receive an ENERGY STAR energy performance score for projects during the design process.

- **ENERGY STAR Energy Performance Scale** – A score between 1 and 100 indicates building performance relative to similar buildings nationwide. Buildings with an energy performance scale score of 75 or higher achieve the ENERGY STAR Building Label, indicating that they perform in the top 25% of their building type.

## Green Globes

The Green Building Initiative developed **Green Globes** as a cheaper, simpler Web-based alternative to LEED. The standards are fairly similar; however, Green Globes is primarily focused on energy efficiency rather than some of the product sourcing criteria in LEED. Green Globes is also more flexible than LEED and allows a greater degree of self-reporting.

## International Facility Management Association (IFMA)

The IFMA provides additional educational resources to help FMs find proven solutions to industry challenges, increase their knowledge base and stay informed about industry trends. The IFMA suite of credentials and professional qualifications provides opportunities for entry into and advancement in facility management. These options represent a full spectrum of professional development for every career stage, from new entrants to experienced practitioners. Their suite of credentials and professional qualifications are as follows:

- **Facility Management Professional™ (FMP®)** – IFMA's FMP is a knowledge-based credential for FM professionals looking to increase their depth-of-knowledge in the core FM topics deemed critical by employers.

- **Certified Facility Manager® (CFM®)** – IFMA's CFM is an internationally recognized credential that sets the standard for ensuring the knowledge and competence of practicing facility managers. It is a competency-based certification that requires ongoing professional development and periodic renewal.

- **Sustainability Facility Professional® (SFP®)** – IFMA's SFP is an assessment-based certificate program delivering a specialty credential in sustainability. By earning your SFP credential, you will develop and gain recognition for your expertise in sustainable FM practices while impacting your organization's economic, environmental and social bottom lines.

- **Essentials of Facility Management® (EoFM®)** – The Essentials of Facility Management is a series of training workshops that describes the field of facility management and its organizational value.

## Institute of Real Estate Management (IREM)

IREM® is an international force of nearly 20,000 individuals united to advance the profession of real estate management. Through training, professional development, and collaboration, IREM® supports their members and others in the industry through every stage of their career.

- **Certified Property Manager (CPM)** – For property and asset managers of any property type who are ready to achieve their desired endgame of lifelong career success.

- **Accredited Residential Manager (ARM)** – For residential property managers newer to the profession and aspiring to take the next step in their careers, and gain control over their future.

- **Accredited Commercial Manager (ACoM)** – For commercial property managers newer to the profession and aspiring to take the next step in their careers, and gain control over their future.

- **Accredited Management Organization (AMO**) – For real estate management firms with a CPM in an executive position and ready to achieve and display company-wide excellence.

## Leadership in Energy & Environmental Design (LEED)

Leadership in Energy & Environmental Design (LEED) is an internationally recognized green building certification system and standard. It delivers third-party verification that a space or building was designed and built using best-in-class strategies to address its entire life cycle. Developed by the U.S. Green Building Council (USGBC), LEED provides building owners and operators with a concise framework for identifying and implementing practical and measurable green building design, construction, operations, and maintenance solutions.

LEED can be applied to all building types and even to entire neighborhoods. LEED rating systems are groups of requirements for projects that are pursuing LEED certification. Each group is geared towards the unique needs of a project or building type. Non-residential building projects can earn any of four levels of LEED certification based on the number of points they achieve, and those 4 levels are: Certified, Silver, Gold and Platinum.

The LEED® rating system has seven areas of concentration; Sustainable Sites, Water Efficiency, Energy and Atmosphere, Materials and Resources, Indoor Environmental Quality, Innovation in Design Process and Regional Priority. Projects obtain credits in these areas to achieve certification. A building becomes certified after receiving a minimum of 40 credits from the USGBC.

There are five LEED building rating systems:

- **LEED for Building Design and Construction (BD+C).**

- **LEED for Interior Design and Construction (ID+C).**

- **LEED for Building Operations and Maintenance (O+M).**

- **LEED for Neighborhood Development (ND).**

- **LEED for Cities/Communities.**

## LEED Professional Credentials – US Green Building Institute (USGBI)

A LEED credential denotes proficiency in today's sustainable design, construction and operations standards. More than 203,000 professionals have earned a LEED credential to help advance their careers. Showcase your knowledge, experience and credibility in the green building marketplace with one of these two LEED professional credentials.

- **LEED Green Associate –** A foundational professional credential signifying core competency in green building principles.

- **LEED Accredited Professional (AP) –** An advanced professional credential signifying expertise in green building and a LEED rating system with specialty in Building Design + Construction, Homes, Interior Design + Construction, Neighborhood Development and Operations + Maintenance.

## Living Building Challenge (LBC)

The **Living Building Challenge (LBC)**, administered by the International Living Future Institute (ILFI), is far more stringent than Energy Star or LEED and must produce at least as much energy as it uses. They are comprised of 20 imperatives to guide projects into the realm of sustainability. LBC is performance-based and, therefore, its outcomes are indicators of success.

## Net Zero Energy Building

The International Living Future Institute (ILFI) provides a certification option for a **Net Zero Energy Building (NZEB)** under its umbrella of the holistic Living Building Challenge (LBC) certification. Such buildings have 100% of their energy needs supplied by on-site renewable energy on a net annual basis.

## Passive House

The **German PassivHaus**, or **Passive House**, rating system is designed to cut energy use by 90 percent. It has none of the other requirements of a Living Building Challenge approach and is all about energy consumption, or the lack thereof.

## WELL

The WELL Certifications focus on people's health and wellness, while LEED is a certification that focuses on environmental impact and sustainability. Both certifications' requirements involve healthy, sustainable construction practices and ongoing building operations after a building is turned over.

- **WELL Building Standard** – The WELL Building Standard focuses on the health and wellness impacts that buildings have on occupants. The standard is arranged into seven areas of concentration, called Concepts and  standard can be applied to a variety of building types, including commercial tenant spaces, existing commercial buildings, hospitality, sports facilities, restaurants, and residential.

- **WELL Health-Safety Rating** – The WELL Health-Safety Rating, an evidence-based third-party designation was created to verify that a building or space has taken the necessary steps to prioritize the health and safety of their staff, visitors, and other stakeholders—ensuring that occupants and visitors entering a certified building—feel more confident in their decision to go inside.

# 15 – Utilizing An ENERGY Savings Plan Budget For Facilities

*Credit: SEBP.*

The future is now for energy savings and energy management and it'ss no secret that a focused, well-defined sustainability strategy, is beneficial to an organization's bottom line. Going green is no longer a fad or a trend, but a course of action for individuals and businesses alike – benefiting the Triple Bottom Line that balances social, environmental, and financial factors.

Today's facility and property managers needs to be able to clearly communicate the benefits and positive economic impact of sustainability and energy-efficient practices, not only to the public, but also to the C-suite. Employees expect their employers to act responsibly, and vice versa, in saving energy.

While there is a dramatic need for each of us–and our organizations–to care for the environment, it is just as important that we convey to executives and stakeholders how these initiatives can benefit our company's financial success. Where better to start than reducing energy costs?

The benefits of energy efficiency don't stop at the meter—they extend to your bottom line. Improved energy performance can boost your net operating income (NOI) and increase your property's asset value. ENERGY STAR calculates that a 10 percent decrease in energy use could lead to a 1.5 percent increase in NOI with even more impressive figures as the energy savings grow.

In light of the current compression of capitalization ("cap") rates (net operating income divided by the sales price or value of a property expressed as a percentage), it is possible to turn pennies into millions. For example, in a 200,000-square foot office building that pays $2 per square foot in energy costs, a 10 percent reduction in energy consumption can translate into an additional $40,000 of NOI. At a cap rate of 8 percent, this could mean a potential asset value boost of $500,000!

## Tailoring the Business Case to Your Organization's Energy Saving Goals

To build the strongest business case for energy savings and efficiency, you should not only leverage the appropriate financial metrics to assess project impacts, but also present the proposal at the right time and in the context of other planned expenditures. Preparing a draft for your CFO's review ahead of time, cementing an ally to save energy costs, and showing how you'll improve your organizations financial bottom line as well as the triple-bottom line—are all wise moves.

With an energy audit and benchmarking report in place, a FM will be equipped with the essential reports and statistics to make their point. Data, reports and energy efficiency is directly tied to lower utility bills and, consequently, lower overall operating expenses.

There are also a host of non-energy benefits to efficiency. A recent study by the U.S. Department of Energy (DOE) found that high-performing buildings are able to demand higher rental rates. They also attract better quality tenants with superior creditworthiness and maintain increased occupancy rates. Although it may be challenging to quantify, efficient buildings increase tenant comfort, improve occupant health, and allow an owner to market the property as sustainable. The resulting increase in overall rental income, in combination with lower operating expenses, means higher NOI.

This translates to increased asset value and a competitive advantage in commercial real estate markets. Energy efficiency offers an opportunity for owners and asset managers to invest in repositioning their building and reduce the associated risk of their investment. Appraisers are increasingly adept at including the value of energy efficiency in their property valuations. This improves an owner's access to favorable financing and underwriting. Finally, strong energy performance is a reflection of excellent building management and can be a key differentiator for a building or an entire firm in competitive markets.

Some financial metrics are more effective than others in evaluating the true costs and benefits of an energy efficient building. It's imperative that efficiency champions communicate efficiency performance metrics in terms that will resonate with tenants and ownership. At the most basic level, this requires translating energy savings from simple kWh or KW to monetary benefits, such as increased rental rates and decreased operating expenses in dollars per square foot.

Many of the most common financial metrics, such as simple payback period, internal rate of return (IRR), and return on investment (ROI) in fact do not capture the full benefits of energy efficient buildings. To build the strongest case for your energy efficiency upgrade or investment, emphasize the following key financial metrics:

- **Net Present Value (NPV)** takes into account the investor's discount rate to calculate how much a cash flow from energy savings is worth in today's dollars, which more accurately reflects the value of efficiency across an efficiency project's payback horizon.

- **Savings-to-Investment Ratio (SIR)** reflects the present value of cash inflows from a project, relative to the present value of cash outflows, which more accurately reflects your return to investment than similar metrics, such as the internal rate of return (IRR).

For more details on how to estimate the costs and savings quickly and easily for a large, complex energy retrofit project at your building, check out the Appendix link for the Spark Tool: A Personalized Business Case to Present to Ownership.

## Investment Analysis and Financing Options if Needed

To implement your action plan, consider taking the following steps:

- Create a Communication Plan—Develop targeted information for key audiences about your energy management program.

- Raise Awareness—Build support at all levels of your organization for energy management initiatives and goals.

- Gain Support From Upper Management – In most companies, it's necessary to gain the support of upper management to move forward with any significant project.

### Create a Communication Plan

Good communication does not just happen. It requires careful planning and implementation. To communicate strategically, you will need to identify key audiences, determine the information that they need, and adapt your messages appropriately for each one. ENERGY STAR offers a variety of communication resources, such as posters and templates that your organization can customize to help you spread the word to employees, customers, and stakeholders. These resources are available on the ENERGY STAR web site.

### Raise Awareness in Your Organization

Everyone has a role in energy management. Effective programs make employees, managers, and other key stakeholders aware of energy performance goals and initiatives, as well as their responsibility in carrying out the program.

Communication strategies and materials for raising awareness of energy use, goals and impacts should be tailored to the needs of the intended audience.

### Gain Support From Upper Management

The most important point of your energy savings plan is to demonstrate how your goals help upper management reach their bottom line. In most companies, it's necessary to gain the support of upper management to move forward with any significant project. Members of upper management are the decision-makers and gatekeepers for making changes.

- **Survey Those Involved –** When attempting to initiate a new project, gather information from those involved in it. Build your case by showing the necessity of a new proposal. Without this evidence, senior management is not likely to see the need for a proposed change.

- **Show the Budget** – If you're suggesting to implement change at work or put a new process in place, show how it will be funded. Senior managers are more likely to support an idea that already has financing in place.

- **Give Them a Choice** - You're more likely to gain upper management support if they feel they had a hand in a decision. When you want to change how something is done, produce more than one solution. More options are better than none.

- **Fit Into Their Goals** – Upper management has its own set of goals and objectives to meet throughout the year. Show how your goals help achieve the bottom line and you're more likely to gain support for an idea.

## Unconventional Opportunities

When searching for project capital, begin by bargain hunting for special programs that support energy performance. Every organization planning an energy performance upgrade should investigate utility incentives, state assistance, and other funding opportunities. A good place to start is the DSIRE - Database of State Incentives for Renewables & Efficiency in the Appendix.

- **Utility Incentives** - Utilities often provide financial incentives for energy-performance upgrades through grants, rebates, fuel-switching incentives, low-interest loans, and energy audits.

- **State Assistance** - Many states offer financial assistance to local governments, nonprofit organizations, small businesses, and other targeted organizations for energy-efficiency upgrades.

- **Foundations and Nonprofit Organizations** - Many foundations and nonprofit organizations sponsor programs that fund energy-efficiency projects.

# 16 – Alternate ENERGY Saving & Sustainability Systems For Facilities

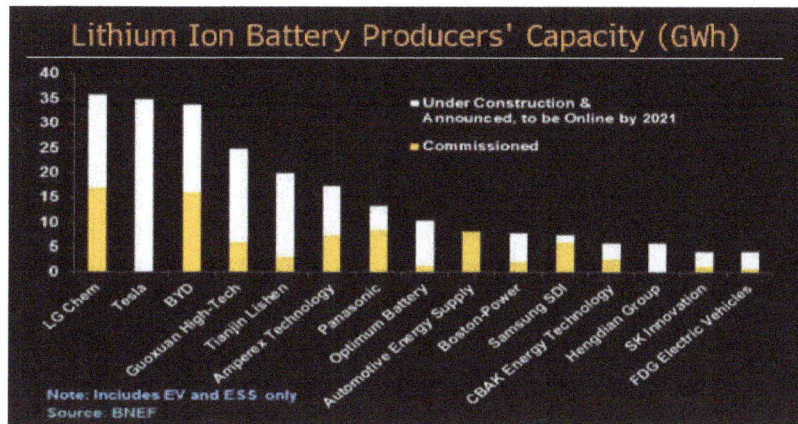

The battery energy storage system (BESS) industry is growing increasingly comfortable with lithium-ion, but its limitations open up a space for other technologies to compete in the storage mix. Back in 2012 and 2013, when Morten Lund, a partner at the law firm Stoel Rives, first began dropping in at energy storage technology conferences, he came across a wide variety of technologies on display.

At the time, lithium-ion was thought to be too expensive, and so there was a lot of mechanical type-storage — pumped hydro and compressed air, for instance, and one technology based on localized compressed water that involved a vertical drill and deep reservoir. There were a number of technologies, Lund said, like the latter, that today are either gone or have become irrelevant.

Per the "Lithium-ion Dominates Utility Storage; Could Competing Chemistries Change That?" article content courtesy of Kavya Balaraman at Utility Dive in October 2020, "All of these things were being proposed almost as equal alternatives . . . it wasn't a given at all that batteries were going to be the answer. It certainly wasn't obvious that lithium-ion was going to be the answer," said Lund.

But fast forward a few years, and the electric utility industry is increasingly turning to battery storage. In 2010, seven battery storage projects amounted to 59 MW of power capacity in the country, according to a recent report from the U.S. Energy Information Administration. By the end of 2018, there were 869 MW of large-scale battery storage in operation in the country, reflecting 1,236 MWh of capacity. More than 90% were lithium-ion systems.

### Other Chemistries Look For Their Own Niche

However, some see downsides to lithium-ion batteries. "Lithium-ion is inherently flawed and I for one can't wait for a better technology to come along and take it down, because it's just not good enough," Stoel Rives' Lund said. He likened lithium-ion batteries to "a delicate flower."

"With lithium-ion, you have the problem where how you use it affects its functionality; in the sense that if you keep running it up and down several times a day, it will degrade and wear out significantly faster than if you don't," Lund said, adding that this makes it difficult to finance standalone utility-scale battery projects.

"I think presenting and developing the business case showing the stacked values that batteries can bring has been something we've had to think outside the box on." Zachary Kuznar, Managing Director of Energy Storage, Microgrid and CHP Development, Duke Energy

In addition, an explosion at an Arizona Public Service storage facility last year raised broader concerns over the safety of lithium-ion facilities, an issue that the industry is working on addressing; in September 2020, for instance, the National Fire Protection Association issued a new standard NFPA 855 addressing fire risk and safety concerns around battery systems.

These challenges, as well as some of the durational limitations of lithium-ion, open up a space for other types of batteries to compete for room in the storage mix of the future.

## Energy Storage System Battery Types and Technology

From the Energy Storage System Battery Types and Technology. Energy Storage Association (ESA) website, the contributions of a number of scientists and innovators created our understanding of the forces of electricity, but Alessandro Volta is credited with the invention of the first battery in 1800.

On its most basic level, a battery is a device consisting of one or more electrochemical cells that convert stored chemical energy into electrical energy. Each cell contains a positive terminal, or cathode, and a negative terminal, or anode. Electrolytes allow ions to move between the electrodes and terminals, which allows current to flow out of the battery to perform work.

Advances in technology and materials have greatly increased the reliability, output, and density of modern battery systems, and economies of scale have dramatically reduced the associated cost. Continued innovation has created new technologies like electrochemical capacitors that can be charged and discharged simultaneously and instantly and provide an almost unlimited operational lifespan. Furthermore, as Energy Storage Systems (ESS) continue to provide a larger share of renewable energy and a variety of battery technologies are being used as follows:

### Lithium Ion (Li-Ion) Batteries

After Exxon chemist Stanley Whittingham developed the concept of lithium-ion batteries in the 1970s, Sony and Asahi Kasei created the first commercial product in 1991. The first batteries were used for consumer electronics and now, building on the success of these Li-ion batteries, many companies are developing larger-format cells for use in energy-storage applications.

There are different types of lithium-ion batteries and the main difference between them lies in their cathode materials. Different kinds of lithium-ion batteries offer different features, with trade-offs between specific power, specific energy, safety, lifespan, cost, and performance. The six lithium-ion battery types are Lithium Cobalt Oxide, Lithium Manganese Oxide, Lithium Nickel Manganese Cobalt Oxide, Lithium Iron Phosphate, Lithium Nickel Cobalt Aluminum Oxide, and Lithium Titanate.

### Redox Flow Batteries

Redox flow batteries (RFB) represent one class of electrochemical energy storage devices. The name "redox" refers to chemical reduction and oxidation reactions employed in the RFB to store energy in liquid electrolyte solutions which flow through a battery of electrochemical cells during charge and discharge.

### Vanadium Redox (VRB) Flow Batteries

The Vanadium Redox Battery (VRB®) is a true redox flow battery (RFB), which stores energy by employing vanadium redox couples (V2+/V3+ in the negative and V4+/V5+ in the positive half-cells). These active chemical species are fully dissolved at all times in sulfuric acid electrolyte solutions. The first operational vanadium redox battery was successfully demonstrated at the University of New South Wales in the late 1980s and commercial versions have been operating on scale for over 8 years.

### Nickel-Cadmium (NI-CD) Batteries

Used in commercial production since the 1910s, nickel-cadmium (Ni-Cd) is a traditional battery type that has seen periodic advances in electrode technology and packaging in order to remain viable. While not exceling in typical measures such as energy density or first cost, Ni-Cd batteries remain relevant by providing simple implementation without complex management systems, while providing long life and reliable service.

### Sodium Sulfur (NaS) Batteries

Sodium Sulfur (NaS) Batteries were originally developed by Ford Motor Company in the 1960s and subsequently the technology was sold to the Japanese company NGK. NGK now manufactures the battery systems for stationary applications. The systems operate at a high temperature, 300 to 350 °C, which can be an operational issue for intermittent operation. Significant installations for energy storage have been used to facilitate distribution line construction deferral. The round-trip efficiency is in the 90% range so provides an efficient use of energy.

### Electrochemical Capacitors

Electrochemical capacitors (ECs) – sometimes referred to as "electric double-layer" capacitors – also appear under trade names like "Supercapacitor" or "Ultracapacitor." The phrase "double-layer" refers to their physically storing electrical charge at a surface-electrolyte interface of high-surface-area carbon electrodes. There are two types of ECs, symmetric and asymmetric, with different properties suitable for different applications. Markets and applications for electrochemical capacitors are growing rapidly and applications related to electricity grid will be part of that growth.

### Iron-Chromium (ICB) Flow Batteries

Iron-chromium flow batteries were pioneered and studied extensively by NASA in the 1970s – 1980s and by Mitsui in Japan. The iron-chromium flow battery is a redox flow battery (RFB). Energy is stored by employing the $Fe^{2+} - Fe^{3+}$ and $Cr^{2+} - Cr^{3+}$ redox couples. The active chemical species are fully dissolved in the aqueous electrolyte at all times. Like other true RFBs, the power and energy ratings of the iron-chromium system are independent of each other, and each may be optimized separately for each application.

### Zinc-Bromine (ZNBR) Flow Batteries

The zinc-bromine flow battery is a hybrid redox flow battery because much of the energy is stored by plating zinc metal as a solid onto the anode plates in the electrochemical stack during charge. Thus, the total energy storage capacity of the system is dependent on both the stack size (electrode area) and the size of the electrolyte storage reservoirs. As such, the power and energy ratings of the zinc-bromine flow battery are not fully decoupled. The zinc-bromine flow battery was developed by Exxon as a hybrid flow battery system in the early 1970s.

# 17 – Emergency ENERGY Power Systems For Facilities

*Credit: Generator Source.*

As California's Public Safety Power Shutoff (PSPS) incidences become more prevalent, energy storage, resource leveling, and back-up power sources are more critical than ever by helping remove facilities from the unreliability of power transmission networks and the high cost of TOU utility rates.

Wildfires are more destructive and deadlier than in the past, and the threat of wildfires is more prevalent throughout the state and calendar year. The overall pattern shows the emerging effects of climate change in our daily lives, particularly in California.

Throughout the year, the California Public Utilities Commission (CPUC) works with CalFire and the Office of Emergency Services to reduce the risk of utility infrastructure starting wildfires, to strengthen utility preparedness for emergencies, and to improve utility services during and after emergencies. Interagency coordination, and cooperation from the utilities is essential when the threat of wildfires is high.

### The "De-Energization" or Public Safety Power Shut-offs (PSPS) Programs

The State's investor-owned electric utilities, notably Pacific Gas and Electric Company (PG&E), Southern California Edison (SCE), and San Diego Gas & Electric (SDG&E), may shut off electric power, referred to as "de-energization" or Public Safety Power Shut-offs (PSPS), to protect public safety under California law, specifically California Public Utilities Code (PU Code) Sections 451 and 399.2(a).

These Public Safety Power Shut-offs (PSPS) programs are a preventative measure of last resort if the utility reasonably believes that there is an imminent and significant risk that strong winds may topple power lines or cause major vegetation-related issues leading to increased risk of fire. Information about the utilities Public Safety Power Shutoff program can be found below.

- Pacific Gas and Electric Company
- Southern California Edison
- San Diego Gas & Electric

# California Braces for More Rolling Blackouts

California is struggling during the summer months to deliver enough power for the first time in nearly two decades as a number of severe heat waves broiled the region, and officials warned of potentially more rolling blackouts if high temperatures persist. The 2020 rolling blackouts are the first to sweep California since 2001.

From the "California Braces for More Rolling Blackouts" article content provided by Katherine Blunt of *The Wall Street Journal* in August 2020:

Both solar and wind power generation systems are unpredictable due to changing weather conditions, and battery energy storage systems are still in their deployment infancy to help solve this problem by supplying stored energy during the peak time-of-use period from 4 – 9 pm. electricity demand when solar energy production is no longer effective or available.

Without sufficient energy storage systems in place to assist and eventually replace the natural gas peaker plants located throughout California along with out-of-state energy source providers, the best that PG&E Corp., California's largest utility, Edison International's SCE, and Sempra Energy's SDG&E can do is urge their customers to reduce power consumption and prepare for rolling blackouts.

The California Independent System Operator (CAISO), which manages the state's power grid, called for utilities to initiate rolling blackouts on Friday and Saturday evening, August 15 & 16, 2020, as demand outstripped supplies during the peak time-of-use period from 4 – 9 pm. Both orders were relatively short-lived, but the emergency measures exposed just how thin the grid's margin for error has become.

**Rolling Blackouts Are Different From Power Shut-Offs**

The rolling blackouts are different from the widespread power shut-offs that occurred in fall 2019 due to the strong winds associated with the fire season. The 2019 power shut-offs were initiated per California's wildfire induced Utility Public Safety Power Shutoff (PSPS) Program which PG&E and SCE each implemented when strong winds increase the risk of their power lines sparking wildfires.

**More Large-Scale and Microgrid Renewable Energy Needed**

California has spent much of the past two decades greening its power supply with large-scale renewable energy, which now supplies more than a third of the state's typical energy needs. The state has almost eliminated coal-fired generation and has been reducing its reliance on natural gas and nuclear power in favor of solar farms and, to a lesser extent, wind power.

Severin Borenstein, a California Independent System Operator board member and energy economist at the Haas School of Business at the University of California, Berkeley, said the blackouts highlight the need for more large-scale batteries to store renewable energy and to deploy it when production is down, as well as larger investments in utility programs designed to encourage customers to conserve energy when necessary.

"As we transition off of fossil fuels, we need to be very realistic about what we're capable of doing," he said. "This should raise more focus on the really disappointing progress we've made on demand response."

### California OKs 'Bridge' Measures to Bolster Grid Against Potential Extreme Circumstances in 2022, 2023

The California Public Utilities Commission (CPUC) in November 2021 approved a suite of decisions aimed at shoring up the electric grid during the summers of 2022 and 2023, in response to an emergency proclamation from Gov. Gavin Newsom.

The decisions, among other things, instruct the state's three investor-owned utilities PG&E, SCE and SDG&E, to collectively procure between 2 GW and 3 GW of additional demand and supply-side resources, expand existing demand response programs by doubling the compensation customers will receive for conserving energy when the grid is strained, and roll out a new energy efficiency program.

Newsom's emergency proclamation, signed in August 2021, sought to free up energy supplies to help ensure grid reliability, including by expediting clean energy projects, streamlining permitting processes, and other measures as reported in the "California OKs 'Bridge' Measures to Bolster Grid Against Potential Extreme Circumstances in 2022, 2023" article content courtesy of Kavya Balaraman at Utility Dive in December 2021.

## California to Pivot to Fossil Fuels to Avoid Blackouts

California is hardly the first state to realize that transitioning to renewable energy is easier said than done. In May 2022, *The Wall Street Journal* reported that energy grid operators across the US were bracing for rolling blackouts heading into the summer. The Associated Press reported that California—a state desperately trying to "quit" fossil fuels—is seeking to tap fossil fuel to avoid blackouts.

From the "California to Pivot to Fossil Fuels to Avoid Blackouts" article by Jon Miltimore Foundation for Economic Education (FEE) in July 2022:

"A sweeping energy proposal Gov. Gavin Newsom signed in 2022 puts the state in the business of buying power to ensure there's enough to go around during heat waves that strain the grid. But some critics say the method of getting there is at odds with the state's broader climate goals, because it paves the way for the state to tap aging gas-fired power plants and add backup generators fueled by diesel."

Unlike most states, California gets most of its electricity—nearly 60 percent—from renewable sources. But the AP notes the state lacks the storage capacity to dispatch sufficient energy when intermittent energy sources are not producing, something Newsom's proposal seeks to address.

The governor's proposal would help "keep the lights on in California," The *Los Angeles Times* notes, "making it easier for solar and wind farm developers to sidestep local government opposition, and limiting environmental reviews for all kinds of energy projects."

The proposal would also likely serve as a lifeline to beachfront gas plants, as well as the Diablo Canyon nuclear plant, the Golden State's largest power plant and only operating nuclear facility.

Newsom has repeatedly called for the phasing out of fossil fuels and denied that doing so would have an adverse economic effect. His pivot to fossil fuels is prudent because it will reduce the dangerous possibility that Californian's will again find themselves without power during the peak heat of summer, but it's also a betrayal ideologically.

For progressives, California is America's energy blueprint, the model showing the way forward on "green" energy. Turning back to fossil fuels is a move that runs against Newsom's own rhetoric and the progressive vision of our energy future. It's an admission that fossil fuels aren't just important but necessary to human survival.

What we're seeing in California is that the tradeoffs of "green" energy are getting real for politicians. Having $7 gasoline is painful, but bearable. Having the highest energy bills in the country is not desirable, but it can be endured. Blackouts are where politicians seem to draw the line, and it's not hard to see why.

Unlike many countries around the world, Americans are not accustomed to blackouts, and it seems the political price to them is simply too high—even for politicians who are green energy evangelists.

## California Wildfires Cancel Out Nearly Two Decades of Emissions Reductions

Fires burned more than 4 million acres, emitting twice as much greenhouse gas the state's total reductions over 18 years. California's record-breaking wildfire season in 2020 essentially nullified nearly two decades' worth of greenhouse gas emission reductions, according to a new study.

The "For the Record: California Wildfires Cancel Out Nearly Two Decades of Emissions Reductions" October 2022 article by Madison Hirneisen and is courtesy of The Center Square's Just the News information bureau, shows how the record-breaking wildfire season, which resulted in more than 4 million acres burned, emitted twice as much greenhouse gas into the atmosphere as the state's total reductions over 18 years, a new study published in the journal of Environmental Pollution.

"Wildfire emissions in 2020 essentially negate 18 years of reductions in GHG emissions from other sectors," the study's authors concluded.

The study highlights that between 2003 and 2019, California's greenhouse gas emissions were reduced by 13%, "largely driven by reductions from the electric power generation sector." But the 2020 fire season alone is "two times higher than California's total GHG emissions reductions," researchers found.

Researchers also discovered that wildfire greenhouse gas emissions are the second "most important source in the state" after transportation and one that "appears likely to grow with future climate change." Between 2000 and 2019, the California Air Resources Board (CARB) said that 41% of the state's greenhouse gas emissions inventory was from transportation.

**All Emissions Must be Considered to Achieve Carbon Neutrality**

A spokesperson for CARB told the *Los Angeles Times* that the agency does not consider wildfire emissions in assessing progress toward greenhouse gas targets because "the targets are specific to human-caused emissions." He told the *Times* that this could soon change, however, because the Intergovernmental Panel on Climate Change has said all emissions must be considered to achieve carbon neutrality.

California officials have acknowledged that climate change is fueling more intense fire seasons across the state. According to Cal Fire, 15 of the state's top 20 most destructive wildfires have occurred since 2015. However, another contributing factor is California's decades long forest mismanagement.

The 2022-2023 state budget included $1.2 billion over two years for wildfire resilience projects, which came on top of a $1.5 billion investment in the 2021-2022 budget.

# 18 – Net Metering For Excess ENERGY Producing Facilities

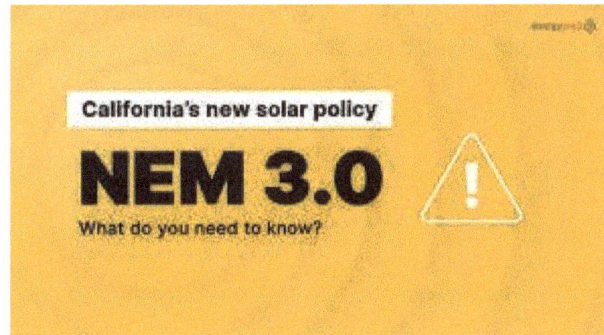

*Credit: Energy Sage blog.*

As reported in the "New Commercial Solar Net Billing Rules for California Investor-Owned Utility Customers - Video Overview EIN Presswire Jan 04, 2023" article in December 2022, the California Public Utilities Commission voted to drastically reduce the value of exported solar energy through new NEM 3.0, aka net billing.

Businesses and residences alike are facing all-time high electricity rates, this paired with growing sentiment for the global climate crisis has forced many to look for alternative solutions that may provide sustainability. Renewable energy solutions like commercial solar and energy storage have shown to be proven investments that not just reduce electricity costs, but provide even more savings throughout the life of the system as electricity costs continue this sky-high trajectory.

**What Is Net Energy Metering?**

Net energy metering (NEM 1 & 2) are key programs that solar solutions have been designed around in California. NEM programs provide value to solar owners who don't need all of the electricity their system produces, awarding retail-value credit for every kilowatt-hour (kWh) sent to the grid. Owners could either exchange those credits for an equal amount of electricity when needed, save credits or roll them over from month-to-month.

Net Energy Metering (NEM) is the difference between energy produced and energy consumed, resulting in net energy. This compensation has helped reduce payback times and increase solar adoption, but IOUs such as Pacific Gas and Electric (PGE), Southern California Edison (SCE) and San Diego Gas and Electric (SDGE) have fought to reduce their costs for the program for years. Even going as far as to request retroactive changes to previous iterations of NEM, potentially going back on their agreements with all existing solar owners.

Thankfully, customers currently with NEM 1 or 2 are locked in for 20 years after the switch to NEM 3 / net billing, which is scheduled for April 13, 2023.

## What Is Net Billing?

Per the "What to Know About The Evolving Economics of Clean Energy Under California's NEM 3.0" Catalyze December 2022 article: Instead of being actively metered, excess solar energy is sold to the grid at a wholesale price. California IOUs will treat all solar energy generators as large-scale energy producers, providing a dollar value based on the avoided cost calculators (ACC) in the final NEM decision.

Each utility offers their own payment schedules for seasonal, weekday and weekend rate structures, but the overall value of solar energy for any installation within an IOU service area seems to have been reduced by about 75%. Below are graphs provided by the CPUC to show how the ACC is calculated hourly and averaged monthly for PGE. The average value of energy is fairly low with spikes to incentivize more energy to be exported to the grid when it is needed.

### How Does Net Billing Affect Solar in California?

The California Public Utilities Commission (CPUC) has designated a 9-year payback period as their target for new solar installations after NEM 3 / net billing begins for new projects after April 2023. Previously through net metering programs, commercial and residential systems in California would average 3-7 years before the savings generated by the system would pay for itself.

According to the wholesale rates provided by net billing, most commercial solar installations will rely on being paired with energy storage systems (ESS) to store electricity and send it back to the grid at night for more value per kWh. Energy storage systems had been paired with solar before but currently face supply constraints that limit access to the technology.

Other net metering programs like net energy metering aggregation (NEMA) and virtual net metering (VNEM) will continue to operate under NEM 2, at least for the next 9 years.

Also taking effect in 2023, a change to California's Energy Code requires both solar PV and energy storage systems for most new commercial buildings, as decided by the California Energy Commission (CEC) for their building energy efficiency standards.

## Key NEM 3.0 Takeaways

California's former net energy metering (NEM) policy, NEM 2.0, offered favorable rates and long-term predictability for new solar systems. In April 2023, California enacted a new market structure, NEM 3.0, which introduces a new set of economics for solar that may necessitate the integration of battery storage and/or intelligent electric vehicle (EV) charging technologies. To secure NEM 2.0's rates and long-term predictability for the next 20 years, applications need to be submitted and completed by the April 14, 2023 deadline.

### What is NEM / Net Energy Metering?

Net energy metering, or NEM, is a billing mechanism that allows utility customers who generate their own solar power to receive a financial credit on their electric bills for excess energy fed back to the grid. For many customers, solar power exported to the grid offsets much of the cost of using utility power, and these savings help in paying off the cost of the solar system installation itself.

On December 15, 2022, the California Public Utilities Commission (CPUC) approved a new set of net energy metering policies, nicknamed NEM 3.0 (also referred to as net billing), which will replace the current rules for new metering, NEM 2.0. The policy will be implemented starting April 15, 2023.

**How is NEM 3.0 Different From NEM 2.0?**

The main difference with NEM 3.0 is that solar export rates will change, becoming much more complicated and requiring increasingly complex strategies and calculations to ensure profitability. On average, the export rate for solar energy could be reduced to a quarter of its current price per kWh.

Under the old NEM 2.0 version, utility customers who generate their own solar power and sell what they can't use back to the grid receive payment at the same, full retail rate that they pay their utility for power. Throughout the year, there are only six different rate periods that need to be considered, allowing for simple, long-term calculations concerning the expected payback time for solar projects.

Under NEM 3.0, the rate that California utilities will pay to people and companies for their excess solar power will be much more variable. There will be 576 different price rate periods throughout the year, determined by different hours, months, and days of the week. These rates will be re-adjusted every other year.

As a result, calculations concerning the payback time for solar projects will be much more difficult to plan around, and on average, rates will be significantly lower.

**How Will My Rates Be Calculated Under the New NEM 3.0 Structure?**

Based on the new rules, the price paid for the export of solar energy will vary based on time of delivery. Rates will be determined by the average hourly Avoided Cost Calculator (ACC), a formula devised by the CPUC and their consulting firm, E3.

The CPUC defines avoided cost as the "marginal costs a utility would avoid in any given hour" if a distributed energy resource provided power instead of the utility. This formula takes into account various factors such as wholesale energy price, transmission and distribution grid costs, and reduced carbon emissions. The ACC's hourly rates are updated every two years.

For commercial building owners who install solar under NEM 3.0, there will be a nine-year period during which export rates for excess solar energy will remain under the same ACC structure. Following the first nine years, customers will face a new set of rates determined by the ACC every two years. This adds a new layer of long term uncertainty when planning for the payback of solar projects. Note that the CPUC has not made a final determination on a new tariff for multi-family properties, so those will continue to receive the existing VNEM tariff for nine years in they apply after the April 15 cut-off date.

**How Does NEM 3.0 Affect My Plans to Install Solar, Storage, and/or EV Solutions?**

For those who plan on installing a solar energy generation system under NEM 3.0, there will now be a strong incentive to install battery storage as well. By storing excess solar energy, utility customers will be able to export this energy at times when it is most financially advantageous, such as peak demand hours during summer nights.

Commercial customers may also take advantage of battery storage to reduce demand charges and participate in other revenue generating programs. Also, building owners who already secured NEM 2.0 rates will be able to install battery storage and take advantage of these benefits without sacrificing their locked-in rates.

There is also an added incentive to utilize more of the energy generated on-site (behind the meter) instead of selling it back to the grid. Because excess power produced on-site will be worth less when sold back to the grid under NEM 3.0, it is advantageous to use more of it on-site, purchasing less of the more expensive energy from the grid.

For example, cold storage facilities who typically do not have excess power to sell back to the grid due to the large energy load of their operations will not feel the impacts of NEM 3.0 as much, as their behind the meter energy use benefits remain. Similarly, if buildings were to install EV charging stations on-site, and power them using their self-generated solar power, this will be advantageous under NEM 3.0, as this is a more efficient use of this electricity than to sell it back to the grid at the new, lower rates.

While battery storage and EV charging technologies will allow commercial buildings to continue to make profitable use of the solar power they generate, the complexity of these strategies will be much more difficult to navigate under NEM 3.0. As electric power moves towards dynamic economics and away from fixed payments, the required calculations for clean energy upgrades will require expertise, experience, and the resources to secure the best fitting solution for each building's characteristics. It will be more important than ever to have a trusted partner for your clean energy solution implementation.

## California Considers Changes That Could Decimate the Rooftop Solar Market

"Net metering, as currently constructed in California, due to the extremely high retail rates that we have, is literally the most expensive strategy for promoting clean energy that we have on the table today," Matthew Freedman, a staff attorney at the Utility Reform Network (TURN), a nonprofit that advocates for the interests of utility ratepayers in California, told Yahoo News. "Retail rates are substantially higher than the cost of new [electricity] generation."

From the "California Considers Changes That Could Decimate the Rooftop Solar Market" article content courtesy Ben Adler, Senior Climate Editor at Yahoo News, in February 2022, TURN argues that it is more efficient to invest in renewable energy at wholesale prices — for example, by building utility-scale solar farms. "We can get way better bang for the buck," Freedman said.

The consumer advocacy group also believes that non-solar customers are getting taken advantage of, pointing to analyses that show the standard retail Californians pay for electricity is 10 percent higher because utilities are compensating for all the revenue lost from solar panel owners by charging more to everyone. Based on that, Freedman counterintuitively maintains that reducing the cost of solar subsidies is actually essential to combating climate change, because higher electricity costs make consumers less likely to switch from fossil fuels to electric cars, stoves and heating systems.

## California's Proposal Has Drawn Criticism From Many Politicians and Activists

California's proposal has drawn criticism from many politicians and activists who are concerned about climate change. Sen. Dianne Feinstein, D-Calif., sent the commission a letter warning that the proposal "may impact the state's conservation goals as we address climate change."

Former Gov. Arnold Schwarzenegger, a pro-environment Republican, wrote in a *New York Times* op-ed that the plan "should be stopped in its tracks" and that the "grid participation charge" is really "a solar tax."

Opponents also say it's unfair to solar consumers who expected to get the retail rate when they bought solar panels. "This is a bait and switch," Jamie Court, a strategist for the nonprofit advocacy organization Consumer Watchdog, told the *Los Angeles Times*. (While the lower rates would apply to all new solar customers, existing solar customers would be allowed to keep the old rate for 15 years.)

Those who want to end net metering say that solar consumers shouldn't get away paying less for grid maintenance because they tend to skew towards wealthier homeowners. "The current Net Energy Metering program disproportionately hurts lower-income Californians who don't own homes and can't afford rooftop solar," Kathy Fairbanks, a spokesperson for Affordable Clean Energy for All, a coalition that includes Pacific Gas & Electric (PG&E), the largest utility company in California, wrote in an email to Yahoo News.

That position has some support in the environmental advocacy community. The Natural Resources Defense Council, for example, has praised the plan.

## Environmental Organizations Are Closer to the Solar Industry's Viewpoint

But most environmental organizations are closer to the solar industry's viewpoint, which emphasizes that solar panel owners do still pay for grid maintenance because they pay the retail rate for the electricity they use, and also that solar customers the costs of grid maintenance and expansion by reducing the amount of electricity needed to generate.

"We support net metering; we support rooftop solar growing in as sustained a way as possible," Laura Deehan, state director of Environment California, an advocacy group, told Yahoo News. "What was proposed here in California would be the most backward-looking policy imaginable from our perspective. Right now, we're racing to get to a 100 percent clean-energy future in our state as fast as possible ... and rooftop solar, paired with storage, is one of the best solutions to the current crisis that we're in."

Deehan also notes that distributing electricity generation across millions of existing homes, rather than building new utility-scale solar in the desert, protects natural areas and makes the grid more resilient to natural disasters, which California is especially susceptible to now because of climate change. Environment California is one of 70 groups that signed a joint letter to Newsom opposing the CPUC's proposal.

"The proposed decision, as it is, has the potential to really decimate the rooftop solar market in California," Katherine Ramsey, a staff attorney for the Sierra Club's environmental law program, told Yahoo News. Ramsey describes the grid participation charge as "very steep" and the proposed reimbursement rate for the energy exported by solar panel owners as "way too low and [it] way too suddenly drops."

"What we have proposed is a gradual transition: more like a ramp as opposed to a steep cliff," Ramsey added. "Both consumers and the solar and storage industry need time to adjust."

# 19 – ENERGY Updates For DERs, Microgrids, SGIP & ESG Programs

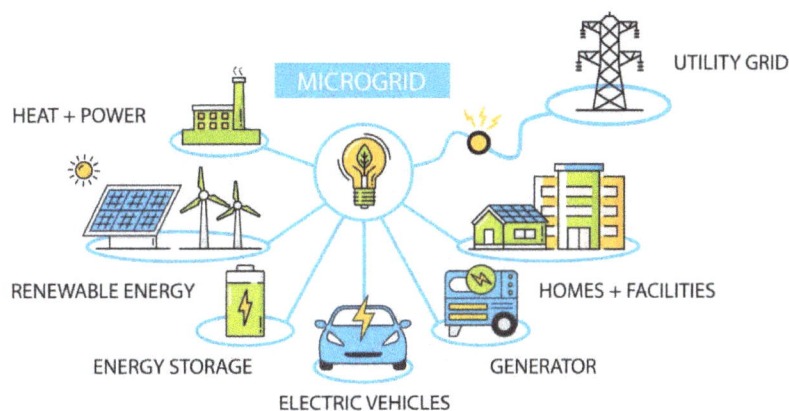

*Credit: Microgrid Knowledge.*

Distributed Energy Resources (DERs), which are defined as distribution-connected distributed generation resources, energy efficiency, energy storage, electric vehicles, and demand response technologies, are supported by a wide-ranging suite of California Public Utilities Commission (CPUC) policies.

The passage of the California Global Warming Solutions Act of 2006 (AB 32) has amplified the need for intensive energy efficiency efforts across California. The California Air Resources Board's (CARB) Draft Scoping Plan for AB 32 implementation states that while "California has a long history of success in implementing regulations and programs to encourage energy efficiency… [it] will need to greatly expand those efforts to meet our greenhouse gas emission reduction goals."

On average, 30 percent of the energy used by commercial buildings is wasted due to inefficiencies. California has taken this principle to heart and with three decades of leadership and innovation in the public and private sectors, California leads the nation, and perhaps the world, in developing and implementing successful energy efficiency efforts.

**Distributed Energy Scores Big Win in US Wholesale Markets with FERC Order 2222**

The Federal Energy Regulatory Commission (FERC) in September 2020, issued Order 2222, its much anticipated ruling that paves the way for aggregated distributed energy resources (DERs) to compete alongside traditional power plants and other grid resources in wholesale markets.

The landmark ruling was heralded in a commission news release as important to "help usher in the electric grid of the future" by removing "the barriers preventing distributed energy resources from competing on a level playing field in the organized capacity, energy and ancillary services markets run by regional grid operators."

Previous FERC Order 841 in 2018 opened wholesale markets to distributed energy resources in general, but Order 2222 in 2020 will now enable these resources to be bundled together into a single bidding entity, opening new possibilities and competitive opportunities.

## What's Included in FERC Orders 841 and 2222

FERC's expansive ruling opens the door to a wide array of technologies to participate. Aggregate resources can be located on a utility's distribution system (or a subsystem) or on-site behind a customer's meter.

Bundled technologies can include energy storage systems (ESS), on-site renewables, energy efficiency, distributed and backup generators, electric vehicles and their charging equipment, and other energy systems common in microgrids. There is no practical limitation on the number of distributed technologies that can be networked together in this manner, and combinations of generation and load modulation can be deployed simultaneously into one unified market offering.

Most notably, this new rule allows several distributed resources to aggregate to satisfy minimum size and performance requirements that they might not be able to attain individually, meaning aggregation can open access to any and all DERs located in competitive markets.

FERC Order 2222 upholds previous determinations that allow resources connected to the distribution grid to serve both retail and wholesale markets, but also directs grid operators to include "narrowly designed restrictions" necessary to prevent double counting of services.

## Microgrids: A Multi-Billion Dollar Opportunity Awaits

Microgrids are integral to initiatives that aim to strengthen the economy, save lives during natural disasters, and make our energy supply more sustainable and our electrical power more secure. Microgrids increasing support more reliable, efficient, and safe power for critical infrastructure.

Local utilities will also still maintain jurisdiction over interconnection of distributed resources to the electric grid, whether or not the resource intends to participate in retail activities. These types of local utility considerations will help prevent legal challenges that bogged down previous proceedings on demand response and energy storage.

The different regional wholesale markets oversee hundreds of millions of dollars in energy transactions every day, and FERC's ruling will open the door for DERs to access those competitive opportunities as noted in the "Distributed Energy Scores Big Win in US Wholesale Markets with FERC Order 2222" article courtesy of Matt Roberts at Microgrid Knowledge published in September 2020.

Previous FERC orders allowing for grid-tied energy storage systems to access limited market opportunities (like frequency response) caused a bit of a battery gold rush in early mover markets like the PJM Interconnection. New wholesale revenue opportunities combined with declining costs and increasing retail value could spur new deployments and accelerate the already burgeoning DER sector.

While the specifics of each market's implementation plans are still months away, FERC Order 2222 is a major win for the DER industry and will have a significant impact on how distributed resources are designed, operated, and compensated for years to come.

# California's Self-Generation Incentive Program (SGIP)

The Self-Generation Incentive Program (SGIP) offers financial incentives for distributed energy resource (DER) systems installed behind the customer meter (BTM) in California. The California Public Utilities Commission (CPUC) opened SGIP in 2001, originally incentivizing solar, biomass generation, and other on-site power sources. Today solar no longer qualifies, and the program has largely refocused on energy storage. To date, the SGIP has contributed to 336 MW of BTM energy storage in California—and it is slated to contribute more.

In September 2018, California Governor Jerry Brown signed Senate Bill 700, which extends the administration of SGIP through 2025 and supplies an additional $830 million in incentives for qualifying BTM technologies. With the federal investment tax credit (ITC) for various DER technologies set to decline starting in 2020, those interested in energy storage and other DER projects in California would be wise to familiarize themselves with SGIP.

**SGIP Program Overview**

Since 2001, the SGIP has evolved significantly. As noted, it no longer supports solar photovoltaic technologies, which were moved under the purview of the California Solar Initiative after its launch in 2006. It has also been modified to include energy storage technologies, to support larger projects, and to provide an additional 20% bonus for California-supplied products.

SGIP was significantly modified by D.16-06-055 to reflect changing conditions and priorities with respect to the program. The changes made by D.16-06-055 include the allocation of 75% of the incentive budget to energy storage projects, capping each technology developer to no more of 20% each of the incentives for large-scale energy storage, residential energy storage and generation, the creation of a step system for incentives and the creation of a lottery system for allocating incentives to projects when a given step is oversubscribed.

**Incentive Structure**

California's SGIP offers incentives to energy storage systems based on several factors, including the kilowatt-hour (kWh) capacity of the system. The incentive amount offered to new storage customers will decline over time as the market matures to ensure efficient use of these ratepayer-funded incentives. Each incentive level is known as a "step," and a certain amount of money is reserved for each step. On a statewide basis, approximately $40 million has been reserved for energy storage systems in each step.

The stated purpose of SGIP has changed since the program's inception in 2001. The program was created as a peak-load reduction program in response to the California energy crisis. In 2009, Senate Bill 412 shifted the program's goal to greenhouse gas reductions. Further changes were made to SGIP in 2016 when the first-come, first-served awards system was modified to include a lottery process, and a majority of its funds were carved out for energy storage projects.

## Energy Storage-Enabled Resilient Microgrid and Island Power Projects

California utilities CPA and SCE have issued requests for microgrid and power resiliency projects using energy storage as the state continues to adapt to an increased risk of power shutoffs. Community choice aggregator (CCA) Clean Power Alliance (CPA) has issued a request for offers (RFO) for developers to build power resiliency backup systems in communities in Southern California.

Per the "Energy Storage-Enabled Resilient Microgrid and Island Power Projects" article by Cameron Murray at Energy-Storage News in January 2023:

The CCA, a non-profit community-owned utility, is seeking the projects through its Power Ready program whereby solar-plus-storage systems are installed at buildings which serve as critical public facilities during outages. The risk of outages has grown with increased wildfires and ageing infrastructure in the state.

The initial phase of the program seeks to have the backup power systems installed at 12 public buildings in Los Angeles and Ventura counties. It will contract with developers on a 20-year build-own-operate model and said it is providing the program at no cost to participating communities, it announced.

The deadline was February 10, 2023, with power purchase agreements (PPAs) set to be signed towards the end of the year. See the CPA's information page for more details.

CPA's RFO is similar in scope to one put out by comparatively larger utility Southern California Edison (SCE), one of the state's big three investor-owned utilities along with PG&E and SDG&E, the week prior.

SCE has launched its 2022 Catalina Island Clean Energy All-Source RFO for the Santa Catalina Island, mainly known as a getaway destination off the cost of LA. The company is seeking energy solutions to serve the island including renewable sources, energy storage, demand response and energy efficiency-based solutions.

The resources will need to come online no later than 2027, and the deadline to submit proposals was May 1, 2023. The island has 4,100 residents as well as commercial and industrial (C&I) customers and around one million annual visitors, SCE said.

Previously-mentioned utility SDG&E has also been working to add microgrid capacity in its areas of service, opting to build four projects in the San Diego region with 180MWh of energy storage capacity last year.

In related news, the completion of two individual energy storage-enabled microgrids in the Sunshine State were announced this week.

The first, from PepsiCo snacking crisps division Frito-Lay (Doritos, Lays/Walkers etc.), saw it complete the transformation of its 1,100-employee Modesto manufacturing facility turned into a showcase of clean energy technologies.

This includes 2.7MWh of on-site battery storage to reduce the site's electricity costs and support grid resiliency through things like peak shaving. It also features a 1MW solar carport combined with an undisclosed amount of energy storage, although that may mean integration with the aforementioned battery storage.

Commercial and industrial-focused (C&I) developer and EPC firm Industrial Power on the same day revealed it had been awarded a construction contract for a 846 kW solar PV, 2.6MWh battery energy storage microgrid in the city of Coachella.

The project will be deployed for Imperial Western Products, a firm which converts waste from the pet, baker and food sectors into sellable products.

## ESG New Year's Resolutions to Help Meet Targets and Establish Leadership

As per the "ESG New Year's Resolutions to Help Meet Targets and Establish Leadership" Catalyze January 2023 post: 2022 was a landmark year for ESG (environmental, social, and corporate governance), as the commercial real estate sector cemented its commitment to not only goal setting, but action.

Sources of pressure to take action continue to expand beyond investors and the public, as regulation mandating emissions reduction for building owners becomes more widespread. Additionally, increasing importance of employee, tenant, and public wellness has placed greater emphasis on the social aspect of ESG, reminding us that ESG is not just about environmental sustainability.

In 2023, the momentum behind ESG will continue to grow, and building owners will need to act boldly and quickly to capture value and competitive advantage. By embracing our recommended new year's resolutions, building owners can not only keep pace with the need for ESG, but emerge as leaders, securing a myriad of financial, reputational, and operational benefits.

**Streamline Your Measurements: Improve Quality and Efficiency of Data Collection**

With the widespread adoption of ESG targets, building owners are realizing the challenges associated with not only meeting those targets, but tracking progress made towards them. Data collection can be particularly tricky when there are multiple activities and technologies being tracked, which may be managed by separate partners who each collect and report their data using different methodologies and platforms, leading to a lack of standardization. Additionally, when it comes to meeting regulatory and financial reporting requirements, the need for accuracy is paramount.

Many organizations are finding the ESG data collection and reporting process to be labor intensive, confusing, and ultimately, frustrating. Yet, it is an essential aspect of ESG action, and is needed to establish baseline metrics and assess the effectiveness of solutions for investors, regulators, and tenants. Without quality data, ESG action loses value, and targets become unattainable.

# 20 – Workforce Development For Sustainable ENERGY Electricians

*Courtesy Newzhawk.com.*

Electricians focus on wiring buildings for electrical power, lighting, or communications systems; they also maintain or repair those systems. They are highly skilled tradespeople who follow regulations and safety standards outlined in the National Electrical Code. Some basic statistics for electricians are as follows:

- Job growth: 7%
- Yearly openings: 79,900
- Earnings: $60K ($28.87 per hour)

The licensing classifications required for California electrical contractors furnishing and installing EV charging stations, battery energy storage, and solar are:

- C-10 - Electrical Contractor
- C-46 - Solar Contractor

Many electricians work exclusively on residential or commercial structures that utilize low-voltage systems. Some specialize in the electrical wiring of factories or electrical equipment maintenance in other industrial settings (such as a power plant). Specially trained line workers work on high-voltage transmission and distribution lines.

To become a licensed journeyman electrician in most states, you'll need to complete an apprenticeship through an electrical contractor, union, or other employer or program that provides paid on-the-job training. Apprenticeship openings tend to be competitive. That's why many students choose to attend a technical or trade school first.

An electrical contractor places, installs, erects or connects any electrical wires, fixtures, appliances, apparatus, raceways, conduits, solar photovoltaic cells or any part thereof, which generate, transmit, transform or utilize electrical energy in any form or for any purpose.

A solar contractor installs, modifies, maintains, and repairs thermal and photovoltaic solar energy systems. A licensee classified in this section shall not undertake or perform building or construction trades, crafts, or skills, except when required to install a thermal or photovoltaic solar energy system.

A pre-apprenticeship electrician program can teach you the basics about electricity, safety procedures, regulations, blueprint reading, tool usage, and much more. With that knowledge, you're more likely to be seen as a good candidate for a paid apprenticeship.

Before the COVID-19 pandemic, California had 537,000 clean energy workers, according to an analysis by the advocacy group Environmental Entrepreneurs. And that number is certain to rise as the state targets 100% climate-friendly electricity and a carbon-neutral economy by mid-century.

## Abundant Opportunities for Electricians in Clean Energy

The clean energy sector offers some of the best job prospects for electricians in the coming years. A 2021 report from the American Clean Power Association projects that by 2030, the 40,000-plus job openings for electricians will outnumber the qualified professionals available to fill them.

The U.S. Bureau of Labor Statistics job outlook data reveals that wind and solar energy jobs are among the country's top five fastest-growing career areas. For the period between 2021 to 2031, employment of solar photovoltaic installers is projected to increase by 27%, and the number of wind turbine technician jobs is expected to increase by a whopping 44%. Both roles involve specialized electrical work, plus other duties depending on the position.

To put these numbers in perspective, the projected employment change for all occupations is 5%, and 7% for electricians for the same period. America, along with much of the rest of the world, is working toward transitioning more and more energy production to renewable sources. This push has created and will continue to generate huge demand for both solar and wind energy careers. If you're interested in joining the field of environmental technology, starting your training as soon as possible can help you capitalize on the demand sooner.

Many electricians will work on solar and wind power equipment, along with other types of electrical work in various settings. This is generally the best option for those who prefer to keep the focus on the electrical work itself. For those who want to do electrical work specific to solar panels, plus other duties related to this form of energy production, training at a solar energy school is worth looking into. Similarly, suppose your interest in wind energy technology goes beyond the related electrical work. In that case, a wind turbine technician training program at a trade school could offer the most direct path to the right career fit for you.

# Electrician Shortage Is Ongoing, Despite Growing Demand

As per the "Electrician Shortage Is Ongoing, Despite Growing Demand" by Lori Lovely in the February 2023 issue of *Electrical Contractor*, twenty years ago, NECA predicted an electrician shortage:

Twenty years ago, NECA predicted an electrician shortage. While demand for electricity escalates, the shortage of qualified electricians worsens. A January 2022 article by Border States notes that the primary underlying causes of this shortage include experienced electricians leaving the field, fewer people entering the field and the lingering effects of COVID-19. The Associated General Contractors of America also predicted that electricians are among the hardest jobs to fill.

According to the Pew Research Center, early retirement of electricians increased in 2020 and 2021, spurred in part by COVID-19. While that trend is slowly passing, with the Bureau of Labor Statistics predicting more workers in 2030 than in 2020, the fact remains that by 2030, all baby boomers will reach age 65 or beyond, draining the pool of qualified electricians.

Compounding this exodus is the lack of interest in skilled labor among the millennial and Gen Z populations. More than 75% of high school and college students want to work in technology, and are more likely to attend college than pursue a skilled labor job. The desire for jobs with flexible hours and potential for remote work often steers them away from trade jobs.

The industry needs to do more than merely replace departing baby boomers. Because electricity consumption is growing as technology focuses on vehicles, devices and buildings reliant on electric power, electrician jobs are growing exponentially.

The U.S. Bureau of Labor Statistics projects growth of electrician jobs by 9.1% from 2020 to 2030, which is higher than the 7.7% growth rate expected for all other occupations. Of all the industries relying on electricians, construction could be hit the hardest by a shortage, because it already employs the highest number of electricians and its expected growth rate over that same period is 9.9%.

Pre-pandemic job projections based on 2019 data predicted there needs to be 808,000 electricians by 2030. While the need for electricians continues, more recent estimates have dialed back that number to 795,700. As the BLS stated, "Demand is the key determinant in explaining future jobs."

Conversely, Rewiring America believes demand will increase, estimating that more than 1 billion machines will need to be installed or replaced in the near future. According to CEO Ari Matusiak, "The scale that is needed to meet the moment when it comes to our climate goals—but also to deliver savings to households and to reinvest in our communities—is pretty massive. And that requires people who know how to do that work."

In answer to the looming shortage, recruitment at the high school level, scholarships to vocational schools, apprenticeships and skilled labor staffing agencies are a few of the tactics being incorporated to encourage an influx of new electricians.

## The California Workforce Development Board (CWDB) Goals for Energy Industries

In June 2020, the California Workforce Development Board (CWDB) submitted a report titled, "Putting California on the High Road: A Jobs and Climate Action Plan for 2030," to the Legislature pursuant to Assembly Bill 398 (E. Garcia, Chapter 135, Statutes of 2017).

Prepared by the UC Berkeley Center for Labor Research and Education, the report offers the State of California a vision for integrating economic and workforce development into major climate policies and programs in order to help achieve California's major climate goals: achieving 2030 greenhouse gas emission reduction targets and transitioning to a carbon neutral economy by 2045.

Carol Zabin, a UC Berkeley labor economist, and the report's lead author, says it's more accurate to talk about "greening" existing jobs rather than creating entirely new "green jobs." Zabin thinks government should craft climate policies that encourage employers in those industries and others to offer high-paying jobs with benefits, make those jobs accessible to non-white workers, and sponsor apprenticeship programs that allow for career advancement.

So, what does the UC Berkeley report recommend? Lots of stuff! It's 636 pages long. Here are a few high-level ideas:

- Public funds should come with strings attached. Companies getting government- or ratepayer-funded contracts to build clean energy infrastructure, such as electric vehicle chargers or public transit systems, could be required to hire from disadvantaged communities, offer state-certified apprenticeship programs and verify their compliance with labor laws.

- Government should partner with industry to fund training programs. The goal should be "comprehensive training that prepares workers for careers, rather than niche programs that train on one particular 'green' skill or 'green' technology that may become outdated as technology advances," the report says.

- Make sure teachers have the clean energy knowledge they need. Instructors at community colleges and apprenticeship programs must be prepared to educate a new generation of workers. State government can help by supporting curriculum upgrades and offering professional development opportunities.

If there's one place the report is relatively sparse on details, it's the section on ensuring a "just transition" for fossil fuel workers. The main recommendation is further study, with a focus on diversifying regional economies that depend on single industries.

## High Road Training Partnerships (HRTP)

One workforce development program with great promise is the High Road Training Partnerships (HRTP) initiative started as a $10M demonstration project designed to model partnership strategies for the state. Including industries like construction, energy, and utilities, the HRTP model embodies the sector approach championed by the Board — industry partnerships that deliver equity, sustainability, and job quality.

Along with these program investments, the Board is producing a body of policy and principle to guide related undertakings across the workforce system. Indeed, the initiative was designed as a campaign — to advance a field of practice that simultaneously addresses urgent questions of income inequality, economic competitiveness, and climate change through regional skills strategies designed to support economically and environmentally resilient communities across the state.

The industry-based, worker-focused training partnerships with a focus on training, apprenticeships, and certifications for California's energy industries, build skills for California's "high road" employers — firms that compete based on quality of product and service achieved through innovation and investment in human capital, and can thus generate family-supporting jobs where workers have agency and voice.

This update was published in the "More Clean Energy Jobs Are Coming: But Don't Call Them Green!" LinkedIn post written by Sammy Roth, *Los Angeles Times* in September 2020.

## How to Get an Electrician's License in California

Whether you are interested in installing brand new electrical systems in homes or businesses or are attracted to the idea of improving things by upgrading wiring and other components in an older system, working as an electrician can be a rewarding career.

Better yet, you may install an electric charging station for a customer's electric vehicle one day and find yourself tracking down a problem with solar power panels not charging an off-grid business owner's battery bank the next day.

Being an electrician gives you an opportunity to help people while making full use of your skills, knowledge, and experience. The rewards include a nice paycheck and a sense of accomplishment in solving problems on the job site.

Now is a great time to consider pursuing a career path to become a certified and licensed electrician. According to the United States Bureau of Labor Statistics (BLS), opportunities for employment as an electrician are projected to grow 9% through 2030.

That increased demand is attributed to anticipated growth in construction, such as through the White House's efforts to rebuild the nation's crumbling infrastructure (which will include thousands of charging stations for electric vehicles).

In addition, more people will be calling on electricians to address the rising need to use alternative energy sources to fossil fuels, such as wind and solar power. But you may be wondering how to get an electrician's license in California.

Becoming an electrician can really pay off for you and your family. In fact, the BLS reported that, as of May 2020, the annual mean wage for electricians in the state of California was $75,900.

**How to Become an Electrician Apprentice**

Before working as a professional, you can work as an apprentice electrician under the supervision of a professional.

To become an electrician apprentice In California, you must be at least 18 years old and possess a high school diploma (or GED), and have earned a grade of "C" or higher in high school algebra (or equivalent) according to Ask the Electrical Guy.

Other prerequisites for entering an apprenticeship include passing an electrician aptitude test (this test can take about 2 ½ hours. You'll also need to undergo an interview and be able to physically do the work involved in being an electrician (so there will be a physical test) and submit to drug testing.

All apprentice electricians in California must have a valid driver's license before they begin.

You can locate an apprenticeship program in the California Department of Industrial Relations (DIR) -- California Electrician Certification Program section in the Appendix:

**How to Become an Electrician**

To work as an electrician in California, you must be certified and licensed. Specifically, you'll need to get the C-10 Electrical Contractor license, issued by the Department of Consumer Affairs, Contractors State License Board, before you can legally bid on any project worth $500 or more.

According to the California Department of Industrial Relations (DIR), if you want to become an electrician, you'll need to do the following:

Begin by registering as an electrician trainee. To do this, you'll need to submit an application, a check for $25, and proof that you are enrolled in an approved school, which offers a DIR-approved Electrician Program. This leading-edge program can prepare you for real-world situations and teach you about electrical theory, national electrical code applications, AC and DC machines and motors, green electricity, commercial installation, electrical circuits, and more.

**How Long Does it Take to Become an Electrician?**

You will need to complete at least 720 hours of electrician instruction from an approved trade school/apprenticeship program that combines hands-on training with classroom instruction.

You will also need to gain 8,000 hours (approx. 4 years) of on-the-job experience (which also can be part of an apprenticeship). This experience must be as a journeyman, or as a foreman, supervising employee, contractor, or owner-builder.

Please note there are no shortcuts here. Working as an unlicensed electrician is punishable by law and not worth the risk. The path to becoming an electrician requires hard work, but it will pay off.

Once you've completed these steps on how to get an electrician's license in California, you'll be eligible to take the state's certification exams (which include a law and business exam and an electrical contractor exam). When you pass these tests, you will receive your electrician contractor's license and be ready to embark on an exciting new career.

The information above was provided by the Summit College "How to Get an Electrician's License in California" article from their website posted in January 2022.

# Appendix

**ASHRAE 1651-Research Project, Development of Maximum Technically Achievable Energy Targets for Commercial Buildings: Ultra-Low Energy Use Building Set:** https://www.ashrae.org/about/news/2016/new-research-from-ashrae-outlines-measures-to-reach-toward-net-zero-energy.

**ASHRAE Standard 90.1-2013, Energy Efficiency Standard for Buildings Except Low-Rise Residential:** https://www.ashrae.org/technical-resources/bookstore/standard-90-1.

**Better Buildings: U.S. Department of Energy:** https://betterbuildingssolutioncenter.energy.gov/challenge?_gl=1*l0q3lj*_ga*MjY1NzUxMzc5LjE2ODQyODMwNzk.*_ga_VEJ5DJ7LND*MTY4NDI4ODA3OS4yLjEuMTY4NDI4ODI0OS4wLjAuMA.

**Building Energy Benchmarking Program: California Energy Commission (CEC):** https://www.energy.ca.gov/programs-and-topics/programs/building-energy-benchmarking-program.

**Building Energy Data Exchange Specifications (BEDES):** https://www.energy.gov/eere/buildings/building-energy-data-exchange-specification-bedes?_gl=1*1y8m58v*_ga*MjY1NzUxMzc5LjE2ODQyODMwNzk.*_ga_VEJ5DJ7LND*MTY4NDI4ODA3OS4yLjEuMTY4NDI4ODIxNC4wLjAuMA.

**California Department of Industrial Relations (DIR) -- California Electrician Certification Program:** https://www.dir.ca.gov/dlse/ECU/ListOfApprovedSchools.html.

**CALSTART Trucks and Non-Road Vehicle Initiative:** https://calstart.org/trucks/.

**DSIRE - Database of State Incentives for Renewables & Efficiency:** https://programs.dsireusa.org/system/program/ca.

**Energy and Facilities Management Software Review:** https://www.softwareadvice.com/.

**ENERGY STAR for Buildings Program:** http://www.energystar.gov/.

**ENERGY STAR Portfolio Manager:** www.energystar.gov/benchmark.

**Energy Use Intensity (EUI):** https://portfoliomanager.energystar.gov/pdf/reference/US%20National%20Median%20Table.pdf.

**Existing Buildings Energy and Water Efficiency Ordinance (EBEWE) Updates:** https://www.energy.ca.gov/programs-and-topics/programs/building-energy-benchmarking-program/local-benchmarking-ordinances.

**Green Button:** https://www.greenbuttondata.org/.

**IFMA 30 Minute ENERGY STAR Webinar:** https://attendee.gotowebinar.com/recording/8637296428037464835.

**PACE - Property Assessed Clean Energy (PACE):** https://www.energy.gov/eere/slsc/property-assessed-clean-energy-programs.

**Putting California on the High Road: A Jobs and Climate Action Plan for 2030:**
https://laborcenter.berkeley.edu/putting-california-on-the-high-road-a-jobs-and-climate-action-plan-for-2030/.

**SGIP - Self-Generation Incentive Program:** https://www.cpuc.ca.gov/sgip/.

**Spark Tool: A Personalized Business Case to Present to Ownership:**
http://betterbricks.org/resources/spark-tool-a-personalized-business-case-to-present-to-ownership.

**Standard Energy Efficiency Data (SEED):** https://www.energy.gov/eere/buildings/standard-energy-efficiency-data-seed-platform.

**U.S. Energy Information Administration (EIA) Electric Grid Monitor:**
https://www.eia.gov/todayinenergy/detail.php?id=40993#.

# Glossary

**Aggregated Energy Resource Solutions (AERS).** An AERS is a system using advanced building energy demand and emulation analysis that balances your energy rate as well as using the lowest rates available.

**British Thermal Unit (Btu):** Standard measure of heat energy. It takes one Btu to raise the temperature of one pound of water by one degree Fahrenheit at sea level.

**Building Energy Benchmarking:** Comparing the energy performance of a building or group of buildings over time (i.e., longitudinal benchmarking), relative to other similar buildings (i.e., cross-sectional benchmarking), or to modeled simulations of a reference building built to a specific standard (e.g., building energy codes). The results can be used to compare energy performance among buildings, identify buildings with the greatest potential for improvement, track energy performance, quantify and/or verifying energy savings, and identify best practices that can be replicated.

**Building Portfolio:** A collection of buildings or facilities owned by a single organization or individual.

**California Independent System Operator (CAISO):** A non-profit Independent System Operator (ISO) serving California. It oversees the operation of California's bulk electric power system, transmission lines, and electricity market generated and transmitted by its member utilities.

**California Power Exchange:** A State-chartered, non-profit corporation which provides day-ahead and hour-ahead markets for energy and ancillary services in accordance with the power exchange tariff. The power exchange is a scheduling coordinator and is independent of both the independent system operator and all other market participants.

**Conservation:** A reduction in energy consumption that corresponds with a reduction in service demand. Service demand can include buildings-sector end uses such as lighting, refrigeration, and heating; industrial processes; or vehicle transportation. Unlike energy efficiency, which is typically a technological measure, conservation is better associated with behavior.

**Corporate Social Responsibility (CSR):** Is the commitment to contribute to economic development while improving the quality of life of the workforce and their families as well as of the community and society at large.

**Cost Avoidance:** Potential savings resulting from energy management measures. Avoided costs are different from cost savings. Cost savings result from reducing spending that is already taking place, while avoided costs demonstrate that future increases in cost will result if the proposed action is not implemented. For example, preventative maintenance on equipment can be thought of as the practice of cost avoidance.

**Demand Response Programs:** Demand response programs are incentive-based programs that encourage electric power customers to temporarily reduce their demand for power at certain times in exchange for a reduction in their electricity bills.

**Demand Side Management (DSM):** A utility action that reduces or curtails end-use equipment or processes. DSM is often used in order to reduce customer load during peak demand and/or in times of supply constraint.

**Dispatchable Generation (or Power):** Refers to sources of electricity that can be programmed on demand at the request of power grid operators, according to market needs. Dispatchable generators may adjust their power output according to an order.

**Distributed Energy Resource (DER):** A non-utility based energy source, typically from a renewable source such as rooftop PV, stationary battery storage or EV battery.

**Distribution Provider (Electric):** Provides and operates the wires between the transmission system and the end-use customer. For those end-use customers who are served at transmission voltages, the Transmission Owner also serves as the Distribution Provider.

**Distribution System:** The portion of the transmission and facilities of an electric system that is dedicated to delivering electric energy to an end-user.

**Duck Curve:** In utility-scale electricity generation, the duck curve is a graph of power production over the course of a day that shows the timing imbalance between peak demand and renewable energy production.

**Energy Cost:** The total cost of energy, including base charges, demand charges, customer charges, and power factor charges.

**Energy Data Analyst:** Conducts energy analysis to support data-driven energy planning and management. The Energy Data Analyst manages internal data resources and provides data collection, analysis, and visualization support. The Energy Data Analyst may also incorporate development of online tools to effectively deliver information and resources to a variety of audiences.

**Energy Efficiency:** A ratio of service provided to energy input (e.g., lumens to watts in the case of light bulbs). Services provided can include buildings-sector end uses such as lighting, refrigeration, and heating: industrial processes; or vehicle transportation. Unlike conservation, which involves some reduction of service, energy efficiency provides energy reductions without sacrifice of service. May also refer to the use of technology to reduce the energy needed for a given purpose or service.

**Energy Information Systems (EIS) and Advanced EIS:** Web-based software, data acquisition hardware, and communication systems used to store, analyze, and display building energy performance data. More advanced EIS offerings provide a higher degree of automated analytics, in combination with baseline models that are used to normalize for key energy drivers such as weather and time of week.

**Energy Manager:** Responsible for the organization's energy management program, activities, and staff. The energy manager sets and/or advises on energy goals; supervises energy efficiency projects and energy-related operations and maintenance activities; oversees energy performance tracking, analysis, and reporting; manages and forecasts energy budgets; and leads a team of energy professionals.

**Energy Service Company (ESCO):** A non-utility entity that provides retail, commercial, or industrial energy services. Also known as an energy service provider.

**Energy Storage System (ESS):** An ESS works by capturing electricity and storing it for discharge when required which allows users to come off the grid and switch to stored electricity, at a time more cost effective to them, giving them greater flexibility and control of electrical usage. Furthermore, at times of high grid power demand an ESS with an excess supply of energy can release stored energy back to the grid, helping to balance it between periods of low energy supply and high energy demand.

**Energy Use Intensity (EUI):** EUI is typically expressed in energy used per square foot of building footprint per year. It is calculated by dividing the total gross energy consumed in a one-year period (expressed in kilowatt-hours or kilo-British Thermal Units) by the total gross square footage of the building.

**ESG:** Is an acronym that stands for Environmental, Social, and Governance and is used as a framework for measuring the sustainability and ethical impact of a company's operations.

**Existing Buildings Energy and Water Efficiency Ordinance (EBEWE):** These ordinances requires existing commercial and multi-family buildings to be benchmarked, audited, retrofitted, and/or retro-commissioned.

**Federal Energy Regulatory Commission (FERC) Orders 841 & 2222:** Requires the removal of barriers to the participation of energy storage in the capacity, energy, and ancillary services markets operated by ISOs and RTOs.

**Gigawatt (GW):** One thousand megawatts, one million kilowatts, or one billion watts.

**Green Button:** A national, industry-led initiative that connects utility customers to energy data using a standard data format. Green Button encourages utilities and service providers to standardize the format of energy data so that customers and third-party service providers can easily access energy usage information from utility suppliers.

**Greenhouse Gas Emission (GHG):** A gas that absorbs and emits radiant energy within the thermal infrared range. Greenhouse gases cause the greenhouse effect. The primary greenhouse gases in Earth's atmosphere are water vapor, carbon dioxide, methane, nitrous oxide and ozone.

**Independent System Operator (ISO):** An independent, federally regulated entity established to coordinate regional transmission in a non-discriminatory manner and ensure the safety and reliability of the electric system.

**Investor-Owned Utility (IOU):** A privately-owned electric utility whose stock is publicly traded. It is rate regulated and authorized to achieve an allowed rate of return.

**Kilowatt Hour (kWh):** A measure of electricity defined as a unit of work or energy, measured as 1 kilowatt (1,000 watts) of power expended for 1 hour. One kWh is equivalent to 3,412 Btu.

**Load Factor:** The ratio of electricity usage to the maximum usage if the power had been left on during a period of peak demand.

**Microgrid:** Is a local electrical grid with defined electrical boundaries, acting as a single and controllable entity. It is able to operate in grid-connected and in island mode. A 'Stand-alone microgrid' or 'isolated microgrid' only operates off-the-grid and cannot be connected to a wider electric power system.

**Net Floor Area:** The gross floor area of a building in square feet, excluding the area of walls and partitions, the circulation area (i.e., where people walk), and the area that houses mechanical equipment.

**Net Metering:** Is an electricity billing mechanism that allows consumers who generate some or all of their own electricity to use that electricity anytime, instead of when it is generated. This is particularly important with renewable energy sources like wind and solar, which are non-dispatchable.

**Operational Savings:** The money saved from operational activities that reduce energy use, such as adjusting equipment set points and operating schedules, turning off lights, and shutting down computers at night.

**Performance Indicators:** A set of quantifiable measures that an organization uses to gauge performance in terms of meeting strategic and operational goals.

**Photovoltaics (PV):** Solar-electric energy cells in any of numerous forms and configurations.

**Power Factor:** Power factor measures the efficiency of electrical power use within a facility's electrical system; it is the ratio between real power (kW) and apparent power (kVA). Commercial customers may be charged a reactive power fee if a facility's power factor is below a certain percentage (e.g., 95%).

**Qualified Balance Resources (QBR):** A QBR system essentially releases stored energy during peak demand and TOU periods after purchasing the facility's peak power usage reserves during the time of day with the lowest TOU rates.

**Rate Schedule/Design:** The rates, charges, and provisions that designate how service is supplied to a class of customers.

**Regional Transmission Organization (RTO):** An electric power transmission system operator (TSO) that coordinates, controls, and monitors a multi-state electric grid. The transfer of electricity between states is considered interstate commerce, and electric grids spanning multiple states are therefore regulated by the Federal Energy Regulatory Commission (FERC).

**Renewable Energy Resources:** Energy resources that are naturally replenishing but flow-limited. They are virtually inexhaustible in duration but limited in the amount of energy that is available per unit of time. Renewable energy resources include biomass, hydro, geothermal, solar, wind, ocean thermal, wave action, and tidal action.

**Renewable Portfolio Standards (RPS):** Also referred to as renewable electricity standards (RES), are policies designed to increase the use of renewable energy sources for electricity generation.

**SMART:** An acronym for Specific, Measurable, Assignable, Realistic and Time-related.

**Stakeholders:** Individuals or groups with an interest in an organization's actions, objectives, and policies. Stakeholders can include staff, program designers, implementers, energy vendors, special interest groups, and customers.

**Sustainable Energy Buildings Plan (SEBP):** A SEBP optimizes an Energy Storage System (ESS) and efficient energy management in support of the primary purpose of the organization. A SEBP has the potential to manage energy resources in a manner consistent with all that is green, zero-net-energy and high-performance.

**Triple Bottom Line (TBL or 3BL):** Is an accounting framework with three parts: social, environmental (or ecological) and financial. Some organizations have adopted the TBL framework to evaluate their performance in a broader perspective to create greater business value.

**Utility Billing Data:** Metered or unmetered utility data that represent electric, water, or gas consumption in a billing cycle. Utility billing data is also used to describe data customers receive from the energy suppliers and payment streams associated with customer accounts. Vendor account details include account numbers, meter numbers, and historical energy-consumption information.

**Zero Energy Building (ZEB):** An energy-efficient building where, on a source energy basis, the actual annual delivered energy is less than or equal to the on-site renewable exported energy.

# References

Adler, Ben. "California Considers Changes That Could Decimate the Rooftop Solar Market." Yahoo News. February 2, 2022. https://news.yahoo.com/florida-and-california-consider-changes-that-could-decimate-the-rooftop-solar-market-experts-say-100018985.html.

Bade, Gavin. "10 trends shaping the electric power sector in 2019." Utility Dive. Jan. 2, 2019. https://www.utilitydive.com/news/10-trends-shaping-the-electric-power-sector-in-2019/545119/.

Balaraman, Kavya. "California OKs 'Bridge' Measures to Bolster Grid Against Potential Extreme Circumstances in 2022, 2023." Utility Dive. December 6, 2021. https://www.utilitydive.com/news/california-oks-bridge-measures-to-bolster-grid-against-potential-extreme/610971/.

Balaraman, Kavya. "Lithium-ion Dominates Utility Storage; Could Competing Chemistries Change That?" Utility Dive. Oct. 15, 2020. https://www.utilitydive.com/news/to-batteries-and-beyond-lithium-ion-dominates-utility-storage-could-compe/586527/.

Benchmarking and Energy Savings. 2019. www.energystar.gov.

Blunt, Katherine. "California Braces for More Rolling Blackouts." *The Wall Street Journal*. August 16, 2020. https://www.wsj.com/articles/california-braces-for-more-blackouts-as-heat-wave-scorches-west-11597613285.

CALSSA Statement on CPUC's Vote to Slash Solar Net Metering. California Solar & Storage Association (CALSSA). December 15, 2022. https://calssa.org/press-releases/2022/12/16/calssa-statement-on-cpucs-vote-to-slash-solar-net-metering.

Cohn, Lisa. "California's Changing Time-of-Use Rates: Calculating the Impact on Behind-the-Meter Solar PV and Energy Storage." Dec. 27, 2018. http://www.realenergywriters.com/blog/2018/12/27/lisa-cohn-enel-x-white-paper/.

Commercial Buildings Energy Consumption Survey (CBECS). 2018. www.eia.org.

Data Trends: ENERGY STAR Certification. 2019. www.energystar.gov.

Energy Management Systems: Maximizing Energy Savings (Text Version). U.S. Department of Energy's Office of Energy Efficiency and Renewable Energy (EERE). www.energy.gov.

ENERGY STAR Building Upgrade Manual. 2008. www.energystar.gov.

ENERGY STAR Guidelines for Energy Management. 2019. www.energystar.gov.

ENERGY STAR Portfolio Manager. 2019. www.energystar.gov.

Energy Storage Investments Boom As Battery Costs Halve in the Next Decade. BloombergNEF. July 31, 2019. https://about.bnef.com/blog/energy-storage-investments-boom-battery-costs-halve-next-decade/?sf106260386=1.

Energy Storage System Battery Types and Technology. Energy Storage Association (ESA). May 14, 2023. https://energystorage.org/.

ESG New Year's Resolutions to Help Meet Targets and Establish Leadership. Catalyze. January 17, 2023. https://catalyze.com/2023/01/17/esg-new-years-resolutions-to-help-meet-targets-and-establish-leadership/.

Froese, Michelle. "BNEF: Energy storage investments boom as battery costs halve in next decade." Windpower Engineering. July 31, 2019. https://www.windpowerengineering.com/business-news-projects/bnef-energy-storage-investments-boom-as-battery-costs-halve-in-next-decade/.

Gheorghiu, Julia. "2019 Power Sector Outlook: Top trends to watch." Utility Dive. Jan. 15, 2019. https://www.utilitydive.com/news/2019-power-sector-outlook-top-trends-to-watch/545995/.

Gheorghiu, Julia. "2019 Solar Outlook: Making ambitious state policy into a reality." Utility Dive. Jan. 9, 2019. https://www.utilitydive.com/news/2019-solar-outlook-making-ambitious-state-policy-into-a-reality/545690/.

Hirneisen, Madison. "For the Record: California Wildfires Cancel Out Nearly Two Decades of Emissions Reductions." The Center Square: Just the News information bureau. October 22, 2022. https://www.thecentersquare.com/california/article_92d236e4-5194-11ed-83e6-832686e79ba4.html.

How to Get an Electrician's License in California. Summit College. Jan. 31, 2022. https://summitcollege.edu/how-to-get-an-electricians-license-in-california/.

Key Takeaways of the Inflation Reduction Act (IRA). Convergent Energy + Power. August 16, 2022. https://resources.convergentep.com/groundbreaking-climate-and-energy-storage-legislation-explained.

Kramer, Ken. "AB 802 Existing Building Energy Benchmarking Law: 5 Biggest Challenges Building Owners and Managers Face." eAudutPro. Feb. 22, 2019. https://eauditpro.com/californias-ab-802-existing-building-energy-benchmarking-law/.

Krieger, Elena, Boris Lukanov and Seth B.C. Shonkoff. "Net Zero Carbon California by 2045: What Will It Take?" PSE. October 2, 2018. https://www.psehealthyenergy.org/news/blog/net-zero-carbon-california-by-2045-what-will-it-take/.

Lopez, Nadia. "Electricity Use Would Surge Under California's New Climate Plan." CalMatters. June 25, 2022. https://calmatters.org/environment/2022/06/california-climate-plan-electricity/.

Lovely, Lori. "Electrician Shortage Is Ongoing, Despite Growing Demand." Electrical Contractor. Feb. 1, 2023. https://www.ecmag.com/magazine/articles/article-detail/electrician-shortage-is-ongoing-despite-growing-demand.

Maloney, Peter. "2019 Storage Outlook: Utility procurement will drive deployments, analyst says." Utility Dive. Jan. 8, 2019. https://www.utilitydive.com/news/2019-storage-outlook-utility-procurement-will-drive-deployments-analysts/545448/.

Miltimore, Jon. "California to Pivot to Fossil Fuels to Avoid Blackouts." Foundation for Economic Education (FEE). July 5, 2022. https://fee.org/articles/california-to-pivot-to-fossil-fuels-to-avoid-blackouts/.

Mulkern, Anne C. "Calif. dilemma: Fight climate change and keep on the lights." Climate Wire. June 6, 2022. https://www.eenews.net/articles/calif-dilemma-fight-climate-change-and-keep-on-the-lights/.

Murray, Cameron. "Energy Storage-Enabled Resilient Microgrid and Island Power Projects." Energy-Storage News. January 19, 2023. https://www.energy-storage.news/california-utilities-seek-energy-storage-enabled-resilient-microgrid-and-island-power-projects/.

Nelson, Mark and Michael Shellenberger. "California's Renewable Portfolio Standard (RPS) Increases Electricity Costs." Environmental Progress. February 12, 2018. https://environmentalprogress.org/.

New Commercial Solar Net Billing Rules for California Investor-Owned Utility Customers - Video Overview EIN Presswire. Jan. 04, 2023. https://ktla.com/business/press-releases/ein-presswire/609519960/new-commercial-solar-net-billing-rules-for-california-investor-owned-utility-customers-video-overview/.

Penrod, Emma. "Wind, Solar to Make Up 70% of New US Generating Capacity in 2021 While Batteries Gain Momentum." Utility Dive. Jan. 13, 2021. https://www.utilitydive.com/news/wind-solar-make-up-70-of-new-generation-in-2021-while-batteries-gain-mome/593278/.

Putting California on the High Road: A Jobs and Climate Action Plan for 2030: California Workforce Development Board (CWDB). UC Berkeley Labor Center. June 2020. https://laborcenter.berkeley.edu/putting-california-on-the-high-road-a-jobs-and-climate-action-plan-for-2030/.

Roberts, Matt. "Distributed Energy Scores Big Win in US Wholesale Markets with FERC Order 2222." Microgrid Knowledge. September 18, 2020. https://www.linkedin.com/pulse/distributed-energy-scores-score-big-win-us-wholesale-markets-wood.

Roth, Sammy. "More Clean Energy Jobs Are Coming: But Don't Call Them Green!." *Los Angeles Times*. September 3, 2020. https://www.linkedin.com/pulse/more-clean-energy-jobs-coming-dont-call-them-green-corey-lee-wilson.

Singer, Stephen. "Energy Storage Made Record Gains in the US in 2022." Utility Dive. March 7, 2023. https://www.utilitydive.com/news/energy-storage-bloombergBNF-factbook-2022/644127/.

Sustainability Guide - EPA'S ENERGY STAR Measurement and Tracking Tool: Portfolio Manager. 2011. *www.IFMA.org*.

Walton, Robert. "2019 Demand Response Outlook: The rise of distributed resources." Utility Dive. Jan. 9, 2019. https://www.utilitydive.com/news/2019-demand-response-outlook-the-rise-of-distributed-resources/545397/.

What is Energy Storage? Enel X. May 14, 2023. https://corporate.enelx.com/en/question-and-answers/what-is-battery-energy-storage.

What to Know About The Evolving Economics of Clean Energy Under California's NEM 3.0. Catalyze. December 16, 2022. https://catalyze.com/2022/12/16/what-to-know-about-the-evolving-economics-of-clean-energy-under-californias-nem-3-0/.

Zahorsky, Darrell. "5 Elements of a SMART Business Goal." BizMoneyTips.com. Aug. 7, 2017. https://bizmoneytips.com/2017/08/07/5-elements-of-a-smart-business-goal/.

Zimmerman, Greg. "What Is the Role of Renewables in Building Electrification and Efficiency?" FM Prime. May 14, 2023. https://www.facilitiesnet.com/energyefficiency/article/What-Is-the-Role-of-Renewables-in-Building-Electrification-and-Efficiency--19837.

# Index

iron-chromium flow batteries · 94

## J

Just the News · 98, 128

## K

Key Performance Indicator (KPI) · 31, 35
Kilowatt hour (kWh): · 124
Krieger, Elena · 9, 128
Kuznar, Zachary · 92

## L

large-scale energy storage · 109
Lawrence Berkeley National Laboratory · 4
LEED (Leadership in Energy and Environmental Design) · 29, 44, 48, 51, 79, 83, 84, 85
LEED Accredited Professional (AP) · 85
LEED building recertification process · 44
LEED Green Associate · 85
Life-Cycle Costing (LCC) · 30
lighting · 26, 42, 55, 59, 65
LinkedIn · 117
lithium-ion batteries · 3, 14, 19, 91, 92
Living Building Challenge (LBC) · 85
load shifting · 21
Lopez, Nadia · 8, 128
Los Angeles Department of Building Safety (LADBS) · 78
Los Angeles Times · 98, 99, 105, 117, 129
Lukanov, Boris · 9, 128
Lund, Morten · 91

## M

Matusiak, Ari · 115
Microgrid Knowledge · 107, 108, 129
microgrids · 21, 107, 108
MicroNOC Inc. · 121
Miltimore, Jon · 97, 128
Mulkern, Anne C. · 10, 128
Mure, Ella · 14
Murray, Cameron · 110, 129

## N

NATE® (North American Technician Excellence®) · 64
National Electrical Code · 113
National Fire Protection Association (NFPA) · 92
National Renewable Energy Laboratory · 15

natural gas · 17, 69
Natural Resources Defense Council · 105
Navigant · 16
near-zero energy buildings · 74
Nelson, Mark · 7, 129
NEM 2.0 · 102, 103, 104
NEM 3.0 · 12, 101, 102, 103, 104, 129
Net Energy Metering (NEM) · 101, 104, 105
Net-Zero Energy Building (NZEB) · 73, 85
New York Times · 105
Newell, Sam · 16
Newsom, Gavin · 10, 97
NFPA 855 · 92
nickel-cadmium (Ni-Cd) batteries · 93
Notice of Proposed Rulemaking (NOPR) · 2

## O

Office of Emergency Services · 95
off-peak hours · 69
Ongoing Commissioning · 44

## P

Pacific Gas & Electric (PG&E) · 8, 14, 19, 70, 72, 95, 96, 97, 105, 110
Passive House · 85
Pathway to Professionalism (P2P) · 81
peak production for a solar PV system · 70
peak shaving · 21
peaker plants · 16, 70
PepsiCo · 111
Pew Research Center · 115
Photovoltaics (PV): · 124
PJM Interconnection · 109
power purchasing agreements (PPA) · 14
Power Ready program · 110
Production Tax Credit (PTC) · 5
Property Administrator Certificate (PAC) · 82
Property Management Financial Proficiency Certificate (PMFP) · 82
Public Safety Power Shut-offs (PSPS) · 95
Publicly Owned Utility (POU) · 78

## Q

Qualified Balance Resources (QBR): · 124
quality installation and maintenance (QI/QM) · 63

## R

Ramsey, Katherine · 106
Ranade, Supria · 2

# Author Bio & Services

*Corey L. Wilson*

Corey L. Wilson is the Founder and President of CLW Enterprises and has been a successful Construction, Project and Program Manager for 30 years for new and remodel educational, medical, commercial, retail, and industrial construction type projects with a combined value of over $150m.

Corey earned a BS in Economics at Cal Poly Pomona in 1985, is a LEED AP (O+M), IFMA Facility Management Professional (FMP), CMAA Certified Construction Manager (CCM), and served as the IFMA Inland Empire Chapter President from 2013 to 2019, and currently Chapter Treasurer.

## CLW Enterprises Services

**Corey L. Wilson, President (951) 415-3002, CLWEnterprises@att.net, www.CLW-Enterprises.com**

### Construction, Project & Program Management

Project Management services for BESS projects; and Construction Management services from the development and design stages to the procurement, construction, and post construction phases using owner partnering and integrated project development for educational, commercial, civic, medical and industrial facilities for new, addition, and remodel type projects of various sizes and complexities, working directly with the project management team and stakeholders.

### Sustainable Energy Buildings Plan (SEBP) Consulting

Sustainable Energy Buildings Plan (SEBP Consulting to attain high performance facilities, reduce utility bills and lower operational costs for sustainable facilities utilizing commercial solar, battery storage, and EV charging station opportunities that contribute to a firm's triple bottom line and a zero-net energy future. Services include working closely with client to assess their energy saving opportunities and developing innovative cost, time, and energy saving solutions as well as self-generation incentive programs (SGIP).

### Energy Sector Workforce Development

Energy Sector Workforce Development is an educational program that provides California's high school, community college and trade/vocational school students as well as transitioning, incumbent and non-renewable energy sector workers essential career information and pathways to prosperity in the energy resource, savings, and sustainability sectors that are critical in meeting California's ambitious 2045 zero net energy goals.

## ENERGY STAR Benchmarking and Certification

ENERGY STAR Portfolio Manager account setup/monitoring and building ENERY STAR Certification services for sustainable energy management tailored to each client's O&M and FM systems needs and requirements to help reduce their energy costs 5% to 10% on average and more. Services include energy consumption analysis, on-site product, technology, and behavior recommendations, and facilitation of energy rebates, grants, and tax incentive programs.

## Facilities Master Planning

Coordinate the Facilities Master Planning (FMP) services team per facility management objectives that are best suited to develop the organizations' master campus planning required for current and future capital improvement project commitments 5 to 10 years into the future. Develop and manage the master facility campus plan, incorporate strategic planning objectives, create tactical work programs, and facilitate stakeholder expectations, as well as environmental, social, and governance (ESG) compliance.

## LEED Building Certifications

LEED Building Certifications featuring the LEED Existing Building Operations + Maintenance (EBOM) rating system to ensure your buildings are meeting California's zero net energy goals, CAL Green / Title 24 code compliance, AB758 - California's comprehensive law on energy efficiency in existing buildings and AB327 regarding solar energy upgrades and net metering; as well as LEED's COVID-19 health and well-being assessments and ratings.

www.ingramcontent.com/pod-product-compliance
Lightning Source LLC
Chambersburg PA
CBHW042353030426
42336CB00029B/3467

9 780999 460399